ARTISTS OF THE NATIONAL LIBRARY OF AUSTRALIA

HAROLD CAZNEAUX

Curated and introduced by Max Dupain

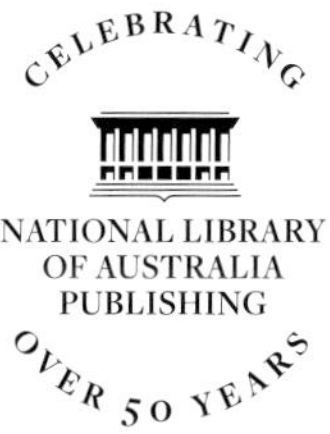

Published by National Library of Australia Publishing
Canberra ACT 2600

ISBN: 9781922507549

The National Library of Australia acknowledges Australia's First Nations Peoples—the First Australians—as the Traditional Owners and Custodians of this land and gives respect to the Elders—past and present—and through them to all Australian Aboriginal and Torres Strait Islander people.

Publisher: Lauren Smith
Managing editor: Amelia Hartney
Designer: Stan Lamond
Image coordinator: Madeleine Warburton

Printed in China by Asia Pacific Offset on FSC®-certified paper.

Find out more about NLA Publishing at nla.gov.au/national-library-publishing.

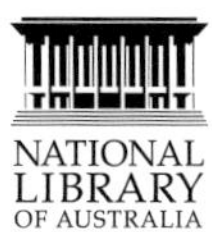

A catalogue record for this book is available from the National Library of Australia

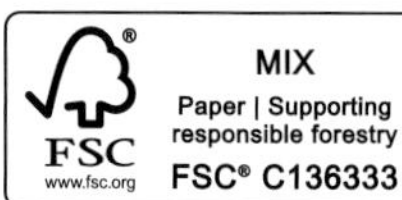

Foreword

For a number of reasons, *Cazneaux* (1978) remains a ground-breaking publication for the National Library of Australia. Yet another significant creative feat of former National Library publisher Alec Bolton, the book married a selection of photographic artworks by 'the father of modern Australian photography' with the evocative words of Max Dupain, a favourite son of Australian photography. Dupain's selection has over time come to define the most well-known and celebrated examples of Cazneaux's work and the Pictorialist aesthetic.

The National Library's Cazneaux collection had been donated some years before in 1972 by his family. This large personal collection of his prints provided the National Library with its first photographic archival material by a photographer of national significance. In curatorial terms, the Cazneaux collection also provided an important counterpoint to the Library's young photographic collection, chiefly comprising examples of the history of photography.

The leader of the Sunshine school of Australian Pictorialist photography, Cazneaux's technical ability with light, focus and angle through the lens, later refined in the dark room, visualised the feelings of the nation, particularly between the world wars. His portraits, landscapes, interiors and streetscapes made the ordinary extraordinary. These were powerful visual statements about Australia, nationhood and life during the first half of the twentieth century.

Fifty years after it arrived at the National Library, the Cazneaux collection continues to sit at the heart of our celebrated photographic collection. This collection today extends to over one million photographs, ranging from digital, through prints and negatives; commissioned series, lifetime archives and the historically significant; and criss-crossing a breathtaking depth of Australian visual social documentary subject matter.

We hope that this new edition of *Cazneaux* in the Artists of the National Library of Australia series encourages new audiences to explore the power and beauty of Harold Cazneaux's Australia.

Nicki Mackay-Sim
Director, Curatorial & Collection Research, National Library of Australia
Canberra, 2024

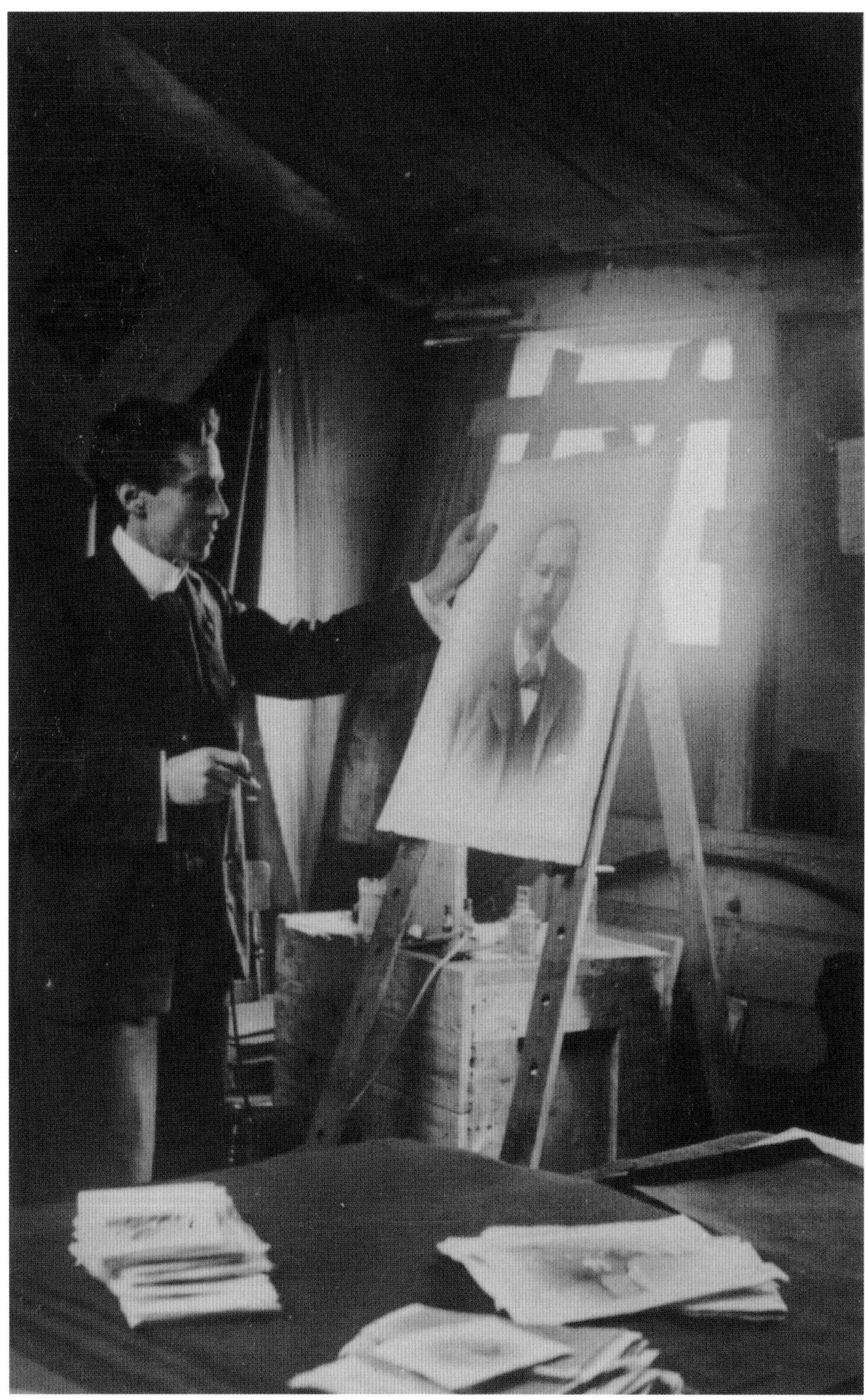

Cazneaux at Freeman's Studios, Sydney 1904
nla.cat-vn1139389

Harold Cazneaux

Harold Pierce Cazneaux was born in Wellington, New Zealand, on 30 March 1878. He was the son of an Australian photographer of French and English descent, Pierce Mott Cazneau (1849–1928), and his wife, Emily (nee Bentley). Pierce Cazneau had been the chief operator at the old-established Freeman's Studios, Sydney, where his wife was a colourist; the firm was noted for traditional portraiture. Cazneau went to New Zealand in 1876 and for a time conducted a studio of his own in a partnership known as Cazneau and Connolly. The family returned to Australia in the late 1880s and settled in Adelaide, where Pierce managed the studios of the American-born Townsend Duryea, and later was manager of another photographic firm, Hammer & Co.

The younger Cazneaux (he added the 'x' to his name in deference to his French ancestry, whereas his father always remained 'Cazneau') began working for Hammer & Co. about the age of 18. He was interested in art, and became a skilled retoucher and colourist. In the evenings, he attended the Adelaide School of Design under H.P. Gill, who was also the teacher of Hans Heysen, a firm friend in later years.

Cazneaux at this time was not attracted to photography, perhaps because it had loomed so large in his family background, or because the conventions of the studios with their props and painted backdrops were not congenial to him. However, in 1898 he saw an exhibition containing work by John Kauffmann (born 1865), a South Australian who had studied photography in England with Horsley Hinton, a pioneer from 1890 of the Pictorial Movement. The aim of followers of the movement was to enhance the artistic qualities of photographs by careful control of detail and tonality during printing. The effect was to make the photograph more like a painting or etching. Kauffmann's work deeply impressed Cazneaux. 'This was my start indeed,' he wrote later. 'The instinctive urge was now fixed in my mind—henceforth my efforts would be towards using photography as a medium of artistic expression and away from the traditional business side of the professional studios.'

Lacking the means to pursue a personal interest in photography, Cazneaux left Adelaide in 1904 to take a better-paid job at Freeman's Studios in Sydney, where he was employed as artist and later as chief operator—the position his father had once held. In 1904, he also bought his first camera, a quarter-plate box camera with which in his spare time and on his way to and from work he began to photograph 'old Sydney', its byways and waterways. At weekends he practised outdoor and informal portraiture using a half-plate stand camera, and at night he worked at the techniques of making artistic prints, of which he became a master; he was especially noted for his bromoils. In 1905, he married Mabel Winifred Hodge, a former fellow worker at Hammer's in Adelaide. They had five daughters and a son.

About 1907, Cazneaux joined the Photographic Society of New South Wales, where his work made such an impression that in 1909 he was asked to give an exhibition. Framed copies of the seventy-five prints that he showed were offered for sale at an average of 35 shillings. Some of the photographs were later accepted at the London Salon of Photography, to which in due course he was elected. In the years that followed, he sent prints to many exhibitions abroad and established an international reputation. He himself never left Australia.

Cazneaux became a frequent speaker on technical subjects at meetings of the Photographic Society of New South Wales, and was soon in demand as a critic. He became a contributor to the Kodak publication *Australasian Photo-Review* (1894–1956), and from 1909 until nearly the end of his life he had work published in the English review of world pictorial photography, *Photograms of the Year,* to which from 1919 until 1952 he contributed an annual review of the Australian scene.

Pictorial photographers in Australia in the 1900s were inspired by the low-toned, sombre work of England and Europe. This was the 'European twilight influence'. Eventually it prompted a reaction from Cazneaux and others, who felt by 1916 that the movement was in the doldrums and who wanted to start an Australian school of thought and action, and to show Australia in terms of sunlight rather than of greyness and what Cazneaux called 'dismal shadows'. In 1916, he and five others founded the Sydney Camera Circle with this aim in view. The group grew to about a dozen invited members, including Cecil Bostock, James Paton, James Stening, William S. White, Malcolm McKinnon, Monte Luke, Henri Mallard and Arthur Ford. They were the priestly caste of the Pictorial Movement in Australia.

By 1918, Cazneaux was ill from overwork. At Freeman's he felt 'sick in health and spirit—fed up with all the artificial make-up of that period of professional portraiture'. He suffered a breakdown and resigned, and it was in this crisis, and from his anxiety for the future of his family, that he decided to set up as a photographer on his own, operating briefly from a small studio in Phillip Street, Sydney, lent to him by Cecil Bostock, and later from his home in the suburb of Roseville, where he had a garden studio and darkroom.

The break from Freeman's was the turning point in his career. He was soon winning a variety of commissions: portraiture, home and garden studies, and commercial work. His innovative use of natural settings and lighting gave his work freshness and spontaneity, though it was always carefully composed, and photographed without waste of plates and film.

In 1919, Cazneaux was approached for work by Sydney Ure Smith, who with Bertram Stevens had founded the periodical *Art in Australia* in 1916, and who was about to launch a high-class social magazine, the *Home*. 'The Bamboo Blind' (page 18) was the frontispiece to the first number, in 1920. The *Home,* which ran until 1942, was a fine medium for Cazneaux's work. His photographs, reproduced usually in sepia on toned art paper, became a feature of the magazine. Through this work he met many artistic, musical and theatrical celebrities, and his commissions multiplied. He dominated the *Home*'s photographic pages to the extent that when it held a competition in 1931 for a social photograph, he carried off the first, second and third prizes. ('Autumn Leaves', page 44, was the second placegetter.)

Cazneaux valued his friendship with Ure Smith more highly than any other association of his professional life. His regard sprang from Ure Smith's acceptance of photography as a form of art. Ure Smith published several photographic booklets with plates by Cazneaux, including *Australia* (1928), *Canberra, Australia's Federal Capital* (1928), *Sydney Surfing* (1929), *The Bridge Book* (1930) and *The Australian Native Bear Book* (1930). Some of these had captions by Ure Smith's editor Leon Gellert, whose choice of the apt phrase Cazneaux greatly admired. A larger work on which he spent much time was *The Frensham Book* (limited edition 1934; republished 1959), containing 100 photographs of life in a girls' boarding school at Mittagong, New South Wales. He later described this as 'the closest I ever got to a personal book'.

In 1934–5, he was commissioned by the Broken Hill Proprietary Co. to photograph the company's steelworks at Newcastle, New South Wales, and its iron mines in South Australia. He was then in his late fifties and had not tackled industrial photography except to record the building of the Sydney Harbour Bridge, but for BHP he produced work of great brilliance, of which 'Steam and Sunshine' (page 16)—more prosaically entitled 'Blast Furnace Plant' in the BHP book *Fifty*

Years of Industry and Enterprise (1935)—is an example. In 1937, he was made an honorary fellow of the Royal Photographic Society.

Most of Cazneaux's daughters worked with him in his Roseville studio ('the Cazneaux family of photographers', they were called), and his son, Harold, acted occasionally as his driver on trips to the country and notably to the Flinders Ranges of South Australia, which Cazneaux visited several times and where he produced some of his best-known studies, including 'The Spirit of Endurance' (page 71).

The death of the younger Harold Cazneaux on war service in 1941 was a heavy blow to his father. Cazneaux at this time felt that his own day was passing. Younger photographers such as Max Dupain and Laurence Le Guay were producing work in a more vigorous style, using bolder methods of lighting and turning out straightforward prints with nothing of the texture and tonality that workers of the Pictorial Movement had striven for. To Cazneaux, a machine age of the camera had arrived. He continued to work through the 1940s, but the best of his photography was behind him.

In October 1952, members of the Sydney Camera Circle and other photographic societies organised a tribute to Cazneaux at the Assembly Hall, Sydney, during which projection-slide copies of his favourite prints were shown to the accompaniment of his tape-recorded comments. In December of the same year, a special 'Cazneaux Story' issue of the *Australasian Photo-Review* was published under the editorship of his friend Keast Burke, with about forty of his photographs and a biographical article by Jack Cato, the Melbourne photographer and historian of Australian photography. Cazneaux had begun writing a series of long autobiographical letters to Cato in 1951, copies of which are now in the National Library. They reflect his modest assessment of his own achievement, an anxiety that other workers of his day should not be forgotten, and a wistful acceptance of newer fashions in photography. Cato based his article for the *Australasian Photo-Review* on them, and reprinted much of it in his book *The Story of the Camera in Australia* (1955; republished 1977).

Cazneaux died on 19 June 1953, and was survived by his wife and daughters.

Alec Bolton
Former Publisher, National Library of Australia
Canberra, 1977

Caz

An appreciation by Max Dupain

I think of him as the father of modern Australian photography. He paved the way, struggling, in somewhat splendid isolation. For company and inspiration he had the English pictorialists of the day like Fred Tilney, Alexander Keighley, Fred Mortimer, F.H. Evans, Horsley Hinton and others; but their influence came over second hand, through third-rate reproduction.

Think of the turbulence of thought and action that hammered out the theories of Post Impressionism and Cubism in Caz's young days, and the later dynamic theories of Dada and Surrealism in both painting and literature. What had we in Australia reflecting these movements, in art or anything else? Practically nothing. In photography we were still tied to the conventions of the old portrait studios with fake and phoney atmospheres, old cameras, head-rests, and stuffed animals for the kids—even Red Riding Hood's wolf!

What a ghastly and depressing environment for Caz's creative soul. It drove him to a physical and nervous collapse.

But his spirit won through; he beat those dreadful circumstances by removing himself and starting out as a photographer in his own right. He had the courage to shed security, even though he carried the responsibility of a wife and large family.

It is from this moment we can trace his development and witness the effect of his having through sheer necessity to handle every kind of subject matter and situation. There was no chance of specialising in any single field in those days. You could be in the middle of a series of home portraits one day and be called upon the next day to cover an industrial complex at night, with an architectural appointment in the city to follow. Your total attitude would have to change, in terms of photographic approach and even of your personal communication with the home-portrait society lady, the foreman engineer and the architect.

What great training it all was for him. With this experience and the knowledge he gained from it, he led the field by the strength of his versatility, his imagination and his technical diligence.

Beneath all the work that he did to keep bodies and souls together, there forever stirred within him the demon which demanded freedom to produce 'pictorial photography'. In fact it was his one-man exhibition of such work in 1909 (the first in Australia) that won him a reputation as a photographer of note and, ironically enough, led to the commercial assignments which followed.

The 'Pictorial Movement in Australia', so often referred to in his letters to Jack Cato, began in England; in isolated Australia, English photography had the greatest influence. Pictorialism represented a narrow and at times bigoted point of view which implied, with its formal rules, that a 'Pictorialist' was not just a simple photographer bent on making the thing work, but a qualified person who would fain rank with the artist and who could speak in aloof terms about chiaroscuro and Hogarth's S curve. The thought of using the camera as an instrument involved with chemistry and optics was abhorrent. Cazneaux quotes an artist writing scornfully in a camera journal in 1899 that 'the Camera is a mechanical instrument for making mechanical pictures for mechanical minds'.

But it is so interesting to note that Cazneaux himself carried his 'Midge' camera to and from work each day, 'over the harbour, in the ferry and through the streets of life and bustle, in sunshine and in rain and through fogs and mists'. Photography was his way of life. His devotion to it was expressed in his revolt against the atmosphere of the studio where he worked and in his urge to come to grips with his real environment. He produced many pictures of city life, and they are the most 'photographic', in my opinion, of all his work. They are the closest he got to the straight documentary approach, and they made a break away from the stereotyped 'pictorial' photograph about which he comments severely in 1916: 'There are so many doing the same thing in the same way'.

He hailed the Sydney Camera Circle as the avant garde movement in Australian photography, hoping that it would 'advance individuality and character in camera work and exploit the sunlight of this country'. It was a worthy enough ambition and the Circle did just that for many years, but the 'pictorial' mood pervaded throughout and to my knowledge the documentary philosophy of photography never got a hearing.

In 1922, Robert Flaherty directed the motion picture *Nanook of the North,* a wonderful and simple story of an Eskimo family and its fight for food. Here the camera was used as a documentary instrument to reveal life in a realistic and vitally human manner. Life itself was the crux of the matter, photography of secondary importance. This film and others like it—*Drifters* by John Grierson, *Moana* by Flaherty—revolted against the synthetic make-believe of the studio, and in its own way Cazneaux's case of rebellion was not dissimilar. But the rebel always remained 'pictorial'. It was his school.

The new documentary philosophy in films had tremendous influence on the still photographers; they began to realise that here was an untapped source of new photographic life. The pretty picture with the art connotation was out and the 'new objectivity' was in. Out of this revolution magazines like *Picture Post, Life* and *Look* were born, and they served to promote some of the greatest photographers of the century. I use the word 'greatest' with the full knowledge that the world in general does not recognise 'greatness' in photography; the 'craft' or 'art' is just not old enough!

I think one of the tragedies of photography in Australia in this formative period was lack of background and an isolation from Europe and America and the great art traditions. We had little or no yardstick against which to measure or contrast our achievements. Caz in his letters recalls 'that great photographer, Stieglitz'; Steichen also gets a mention and so does Baron De Meyer, the fashion photographer. He does not tell us that Stieglitz opened the Photo-Secession Gallery in New York in 1905 and showed the public for the first time the work of the Cubists, the Fauves, Picasso, and many other revolutionary painters and sculptors. He mixed painting and photography in exhibitions. Edward Steichen's work was shown there and 'Gallery 291' was a meeting place of the avant garde in art and photography. What mental stimulation!

Obviously we had not heard about those developments in Australia, any more than we heard about Edward Weston when later he was working at Point Lobos, California, and in the sand dunes in Death Valley. These devoted people had no influence on Australian photography until the 1930s. I have not forgotten Eugene Atget, probably the greatest of them all, who set out between 1898 and 1927 to photograph Paris. He left an enormous collection of photographs of buildings, staircases, door-knockers, ornate stucco decoration, shop fronts and vehicles. He was unregarded in his own lifetime and died in poverty, leaving to posterity nearly ten thousand documents of Paris. How insular we really were in this country.

But admitting all this, we have to thank Harold Cazneaux for so much. His work is what matters, its place in the history of Australian photography and its influence on past, present and future generations of photographers.

Let us look at and think about his pictures. There is much photography done today that can only be classed as proletarian. Cazneaux's work is not proletarian, it is elitist. His trees are not objective renderings of trees, they are symbols of power and endurance. His portraits of women are essentially soft and feminine, and his male portraits are straightforwardly masculine. The machines in his industrial work are eulogised and become dramatic presentations of functional forms. There is always aspiration and a reaching beyond life to something idealistic and finer than the life man makes for himself on this earth. All that has now changed. Today we are concerned with the commonplace, the rational, the actual, the objective, the remorseless presentation of any act of life. Maybe this is what photography is all about. We will not be certain for another hundred years.

The landscapes must be looked at first. I think they were dearest to Caz's heart notwithstanding his fluent versatility in other fields. There is a serenity about them, the poetic silence of sunlit afternoons. No jarring note occurs anywhere and the masses are arranged with creative selectivity, in good common-sense terms, which makes each picture easy to comprehend at once. They are painterly in a photographic way, and there is a romantic purity in the long shots that gives the mind and eye a great sense of relief: the escape, if you like, into the inherent spaces of nature. Light, form, texture and movement make up the synthesis of these pictures, with an occasional dramatic punctuation from the Flinders Ranges—'Spirit of Endurance' is heroic in stature and endeavour.

The portraits are almost another world. Notice the action in most of them: Julian Ashton demonstrating, Norman Lindsay etching, George Lambert intent on a sculpture, Henry Gibbons drawing, the anaesthetist working with concentration and concern. This is good practice, to have the subject relaxed in his own familiar context. The child portraits, especially the double heads, recall Julia Margaret Cameron's work of the 1860s. The sun-striped pictures have a magazine flavour because they are eye-catching and stand apart from the somewhat formal style of the other work.

The beautiful and wistful portrait of Anna Pavlova is sensitively approached and is as simple in presentation as possible. The portrait photograph feeds on the subject, and most of these people are celebrated. There is extra fundamental interest on that account. But wisely Caz has left it at that; the character comes over without prompting, without staging any effect of lighting or background (except the zebra of 'Pergola Pattern').

There is drama in the industrial shots. The machine forms, so welcome and familiar to me, show up in opposing lines of broad silhouette. The figures of men give scale to the total assemblage. How is it that such a colossus as BHP's steelworks, the very sound and fury of it, can be transmitted in a Cazneaux photograph, not only as an illustration but as an electrifying mystery of awe and strength!

The architectural photographs show buildings of grand dimension (for Australia!). Cazneaux with his sense of the symmetrical has made balanced pictures of the great staircase of Elizabeth Bay House and the entrance porch of Greystanes (now no more). Hardy Wilson, probably Australia's greatest draughtsman, selected the same viewpoint of the latter.

There are play shots like 'The Razzle Dazzle'—almost documentary but without the accidental touch. But there is great movement in the simplified wheel. Not the whole wheel, take note, but a segment of it, seen close up and intensified. 'Sydney Surfing' must have been a star shot in the days of 1929. It is a view from above that emphasises the pattern and movement of the wave with everybody drowning therein! And there is a Gertrude Kasebier picture of a Victorian lady holding a door open at the approach of a man; a beautiful shot against the light, full of mystery and promise. (But maybe it's only the plumber!) Note the Victorian atmosphere, the turned timber curtain rail and rings, the book on the windowsill.

I can't help recalling one man's name that occurs again and again in Caz's letters to Jack Cato: that of Sydney Ure Smith. No tribute can be too high or too glowing for this great lover and promoter of art and photography in Australia. Without being authoritarian in any way whatsoever, he influenced our art world as much as Julian Ashton. I share, wholeheartedly, Caz's admiration of and gratitude to him.

Let us finish on a humble note by quoting Harold Cazneaux: 'I do not wish to dwell on the subject of the status of photography as an art—just let us all go forward doing our work sincerely and soundly—the results will speak for themselves'.

For me that is just right: 'Don't talk—do!'

Max Dupain
Sydney, 1978

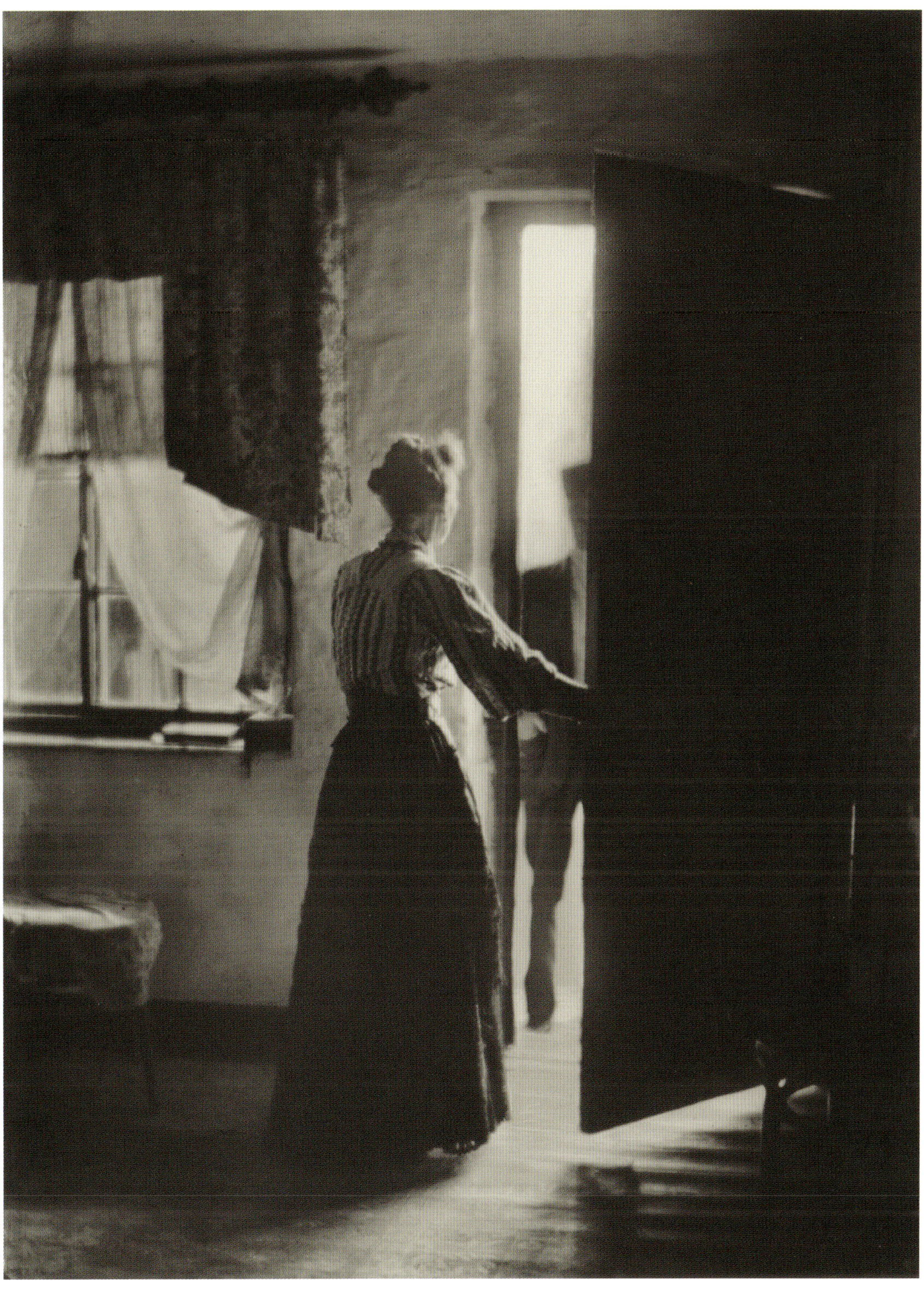

Come In, Old Sydney 1908
nla.cat-vn282646

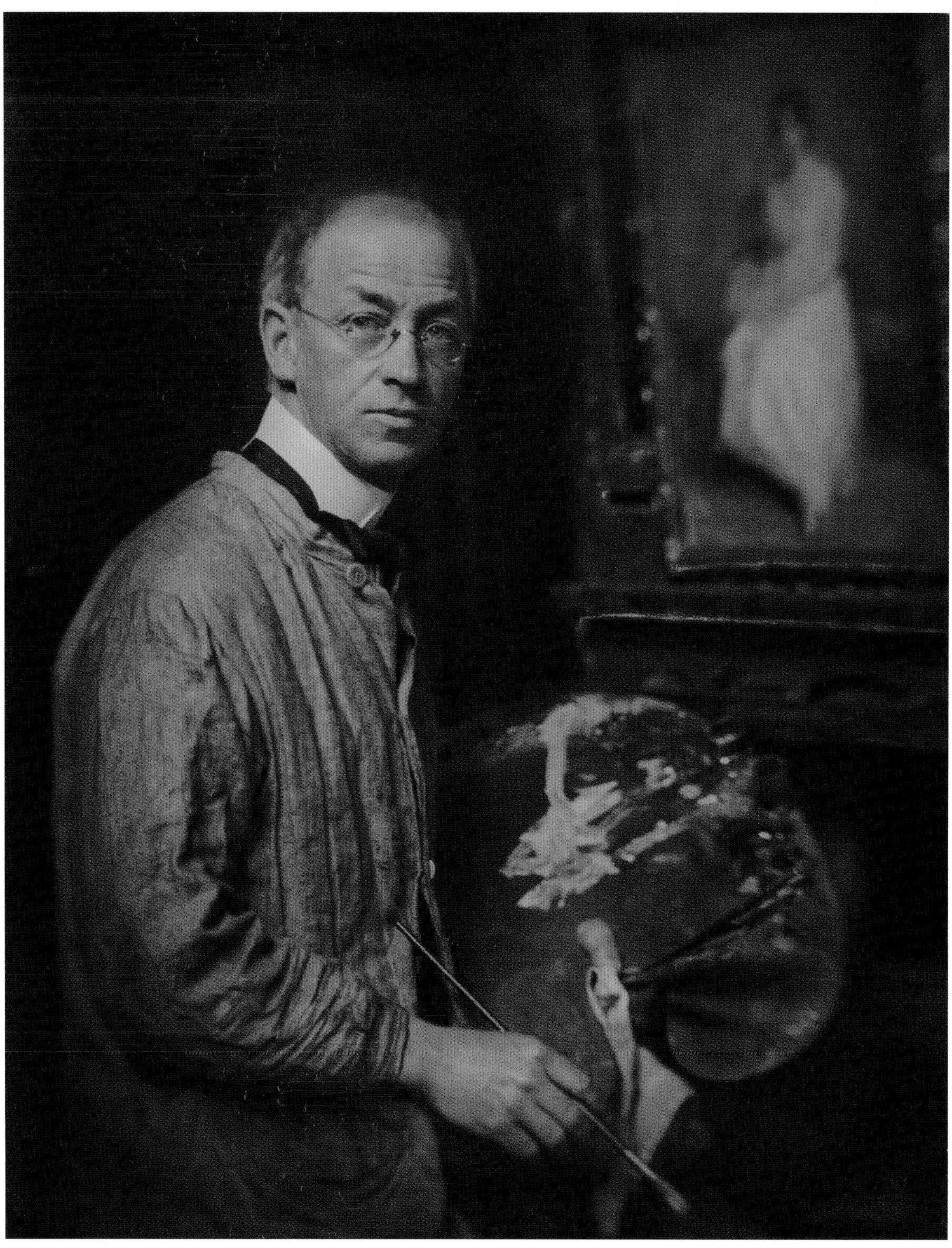

Norman Carter, Artist 1924
nla.cat-vn1986795

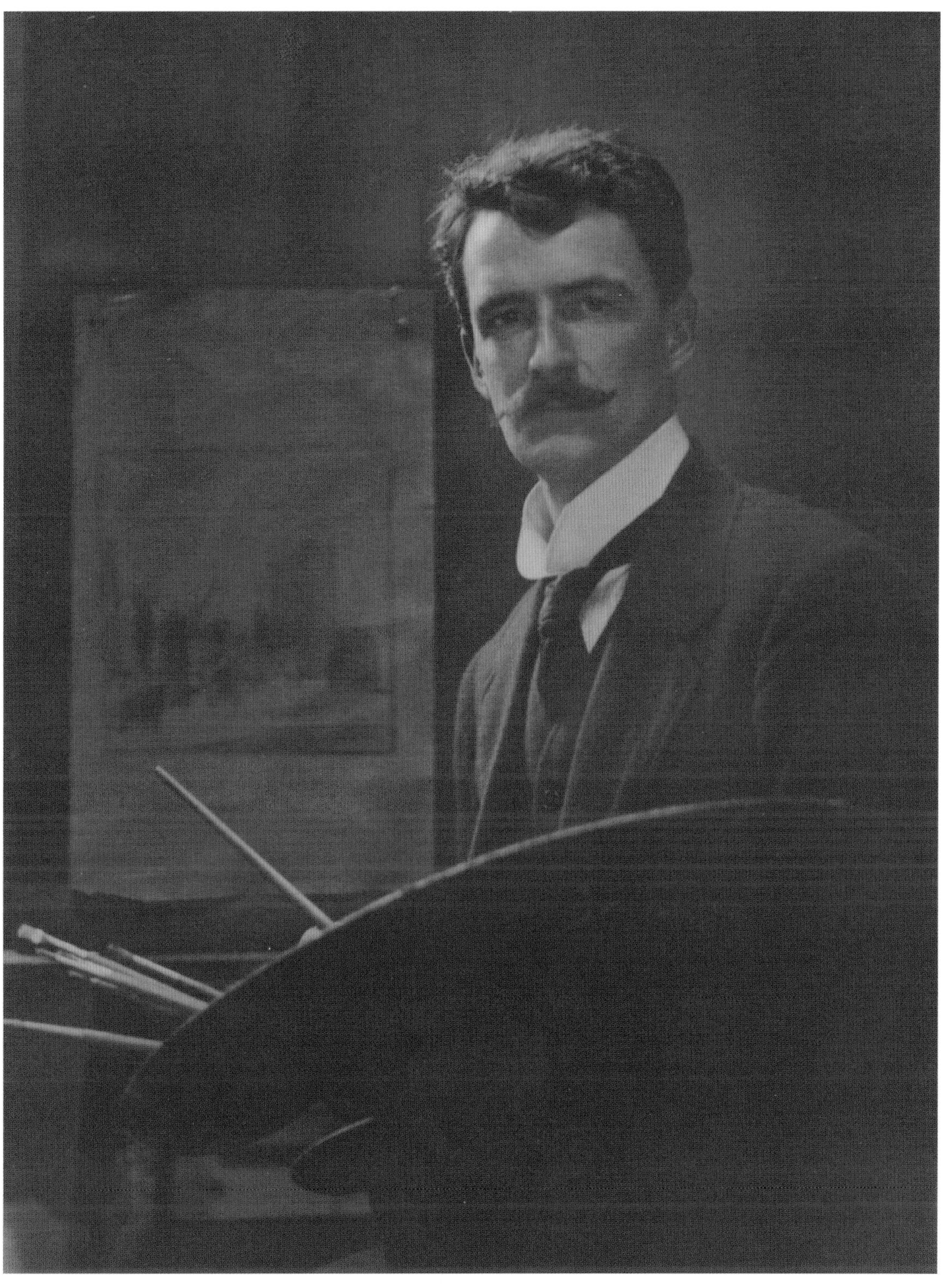

The Artist: Portrait of Leslie H. Beer c.1908
nla.cat-vn1986785

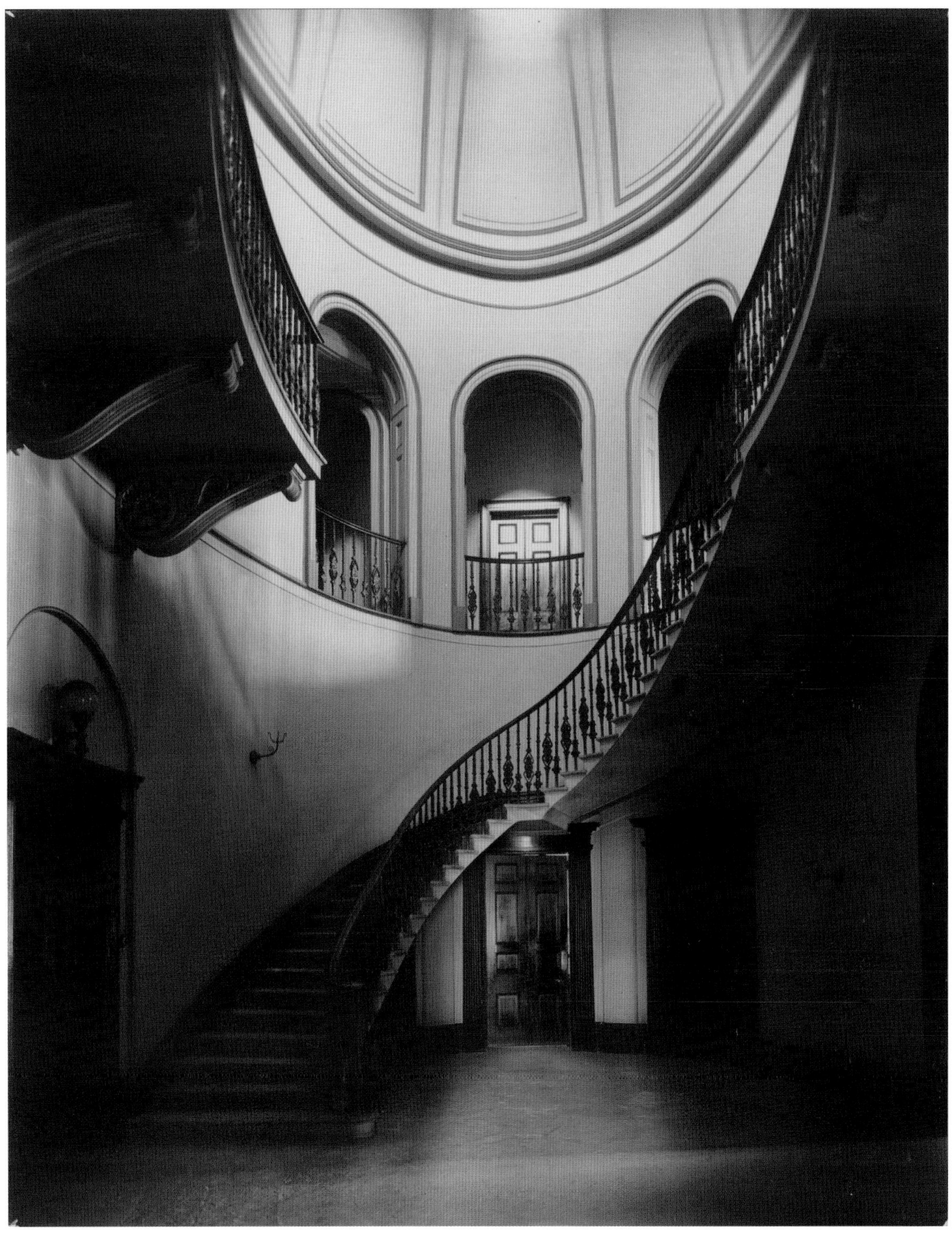

Staircase, Elizabeth Bay House, Sydney 1930
nla.cat-vn463588

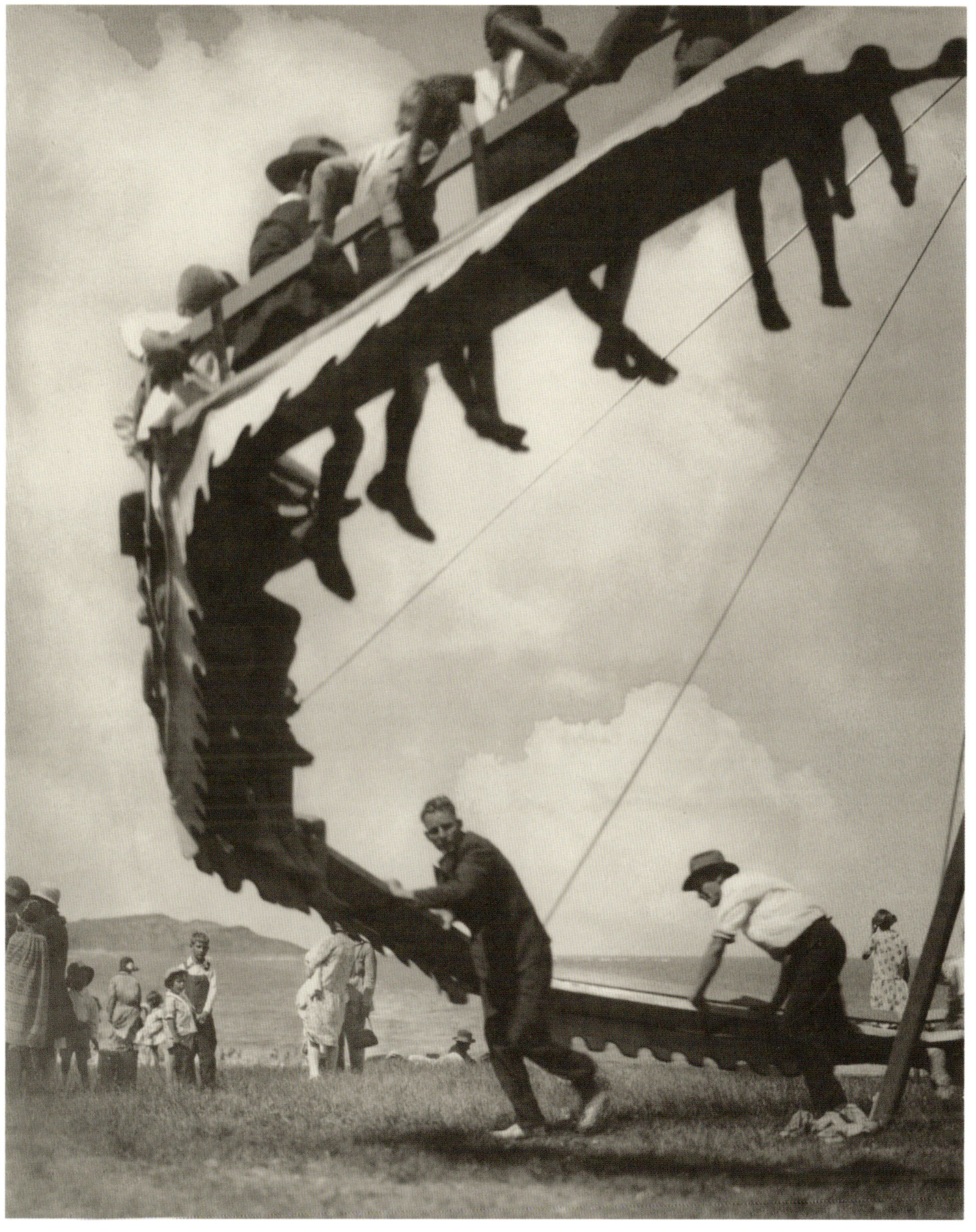

The Wheel of Youth 1929
nla.cat-vn463338

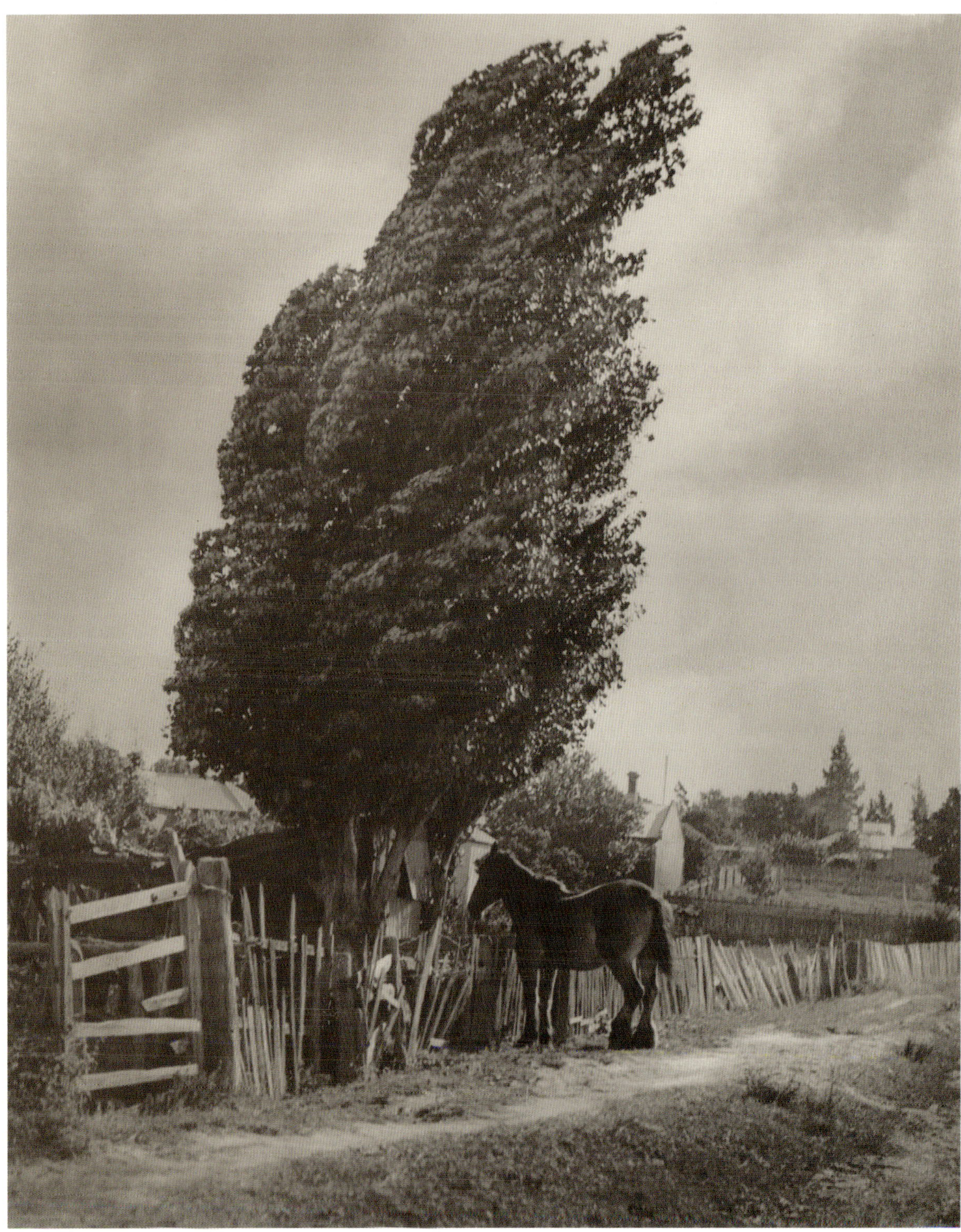

Windy Day between 1910 and 1927
nla.cat-vn464870

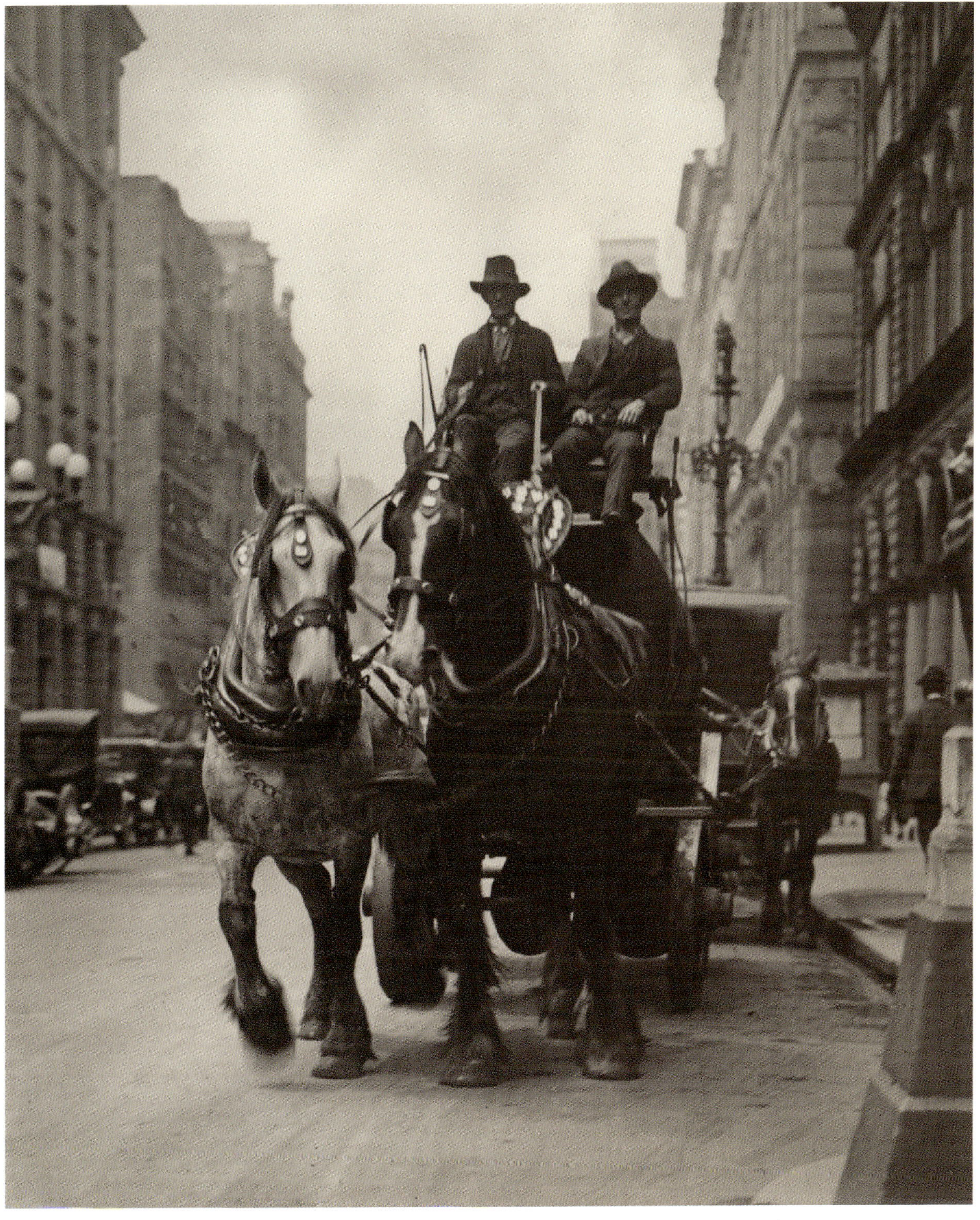

Kings of the Road c.1920s
nla.cat-vn1963778

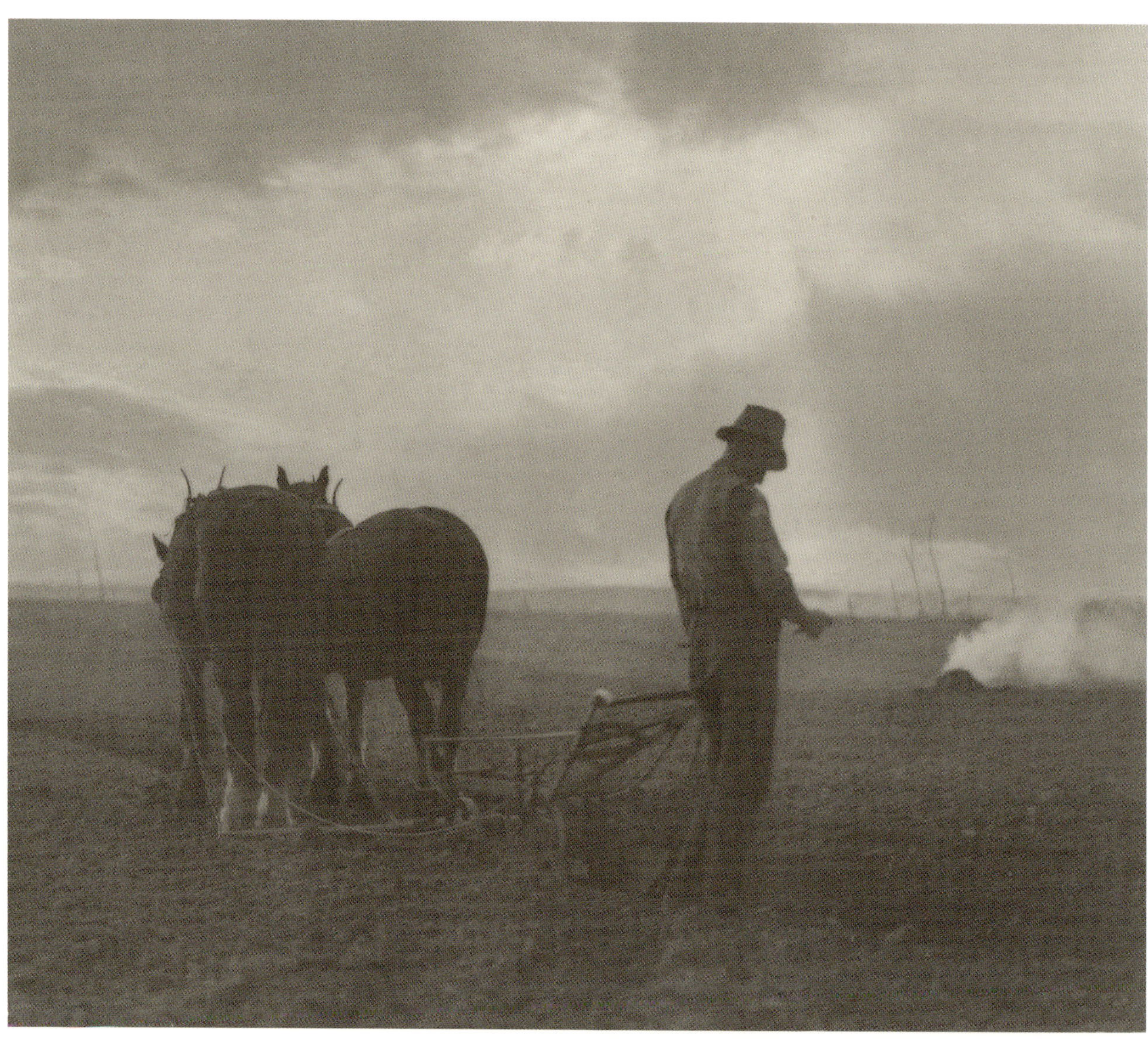

Peace after War and Memories 1918
nla.cat-vn465033

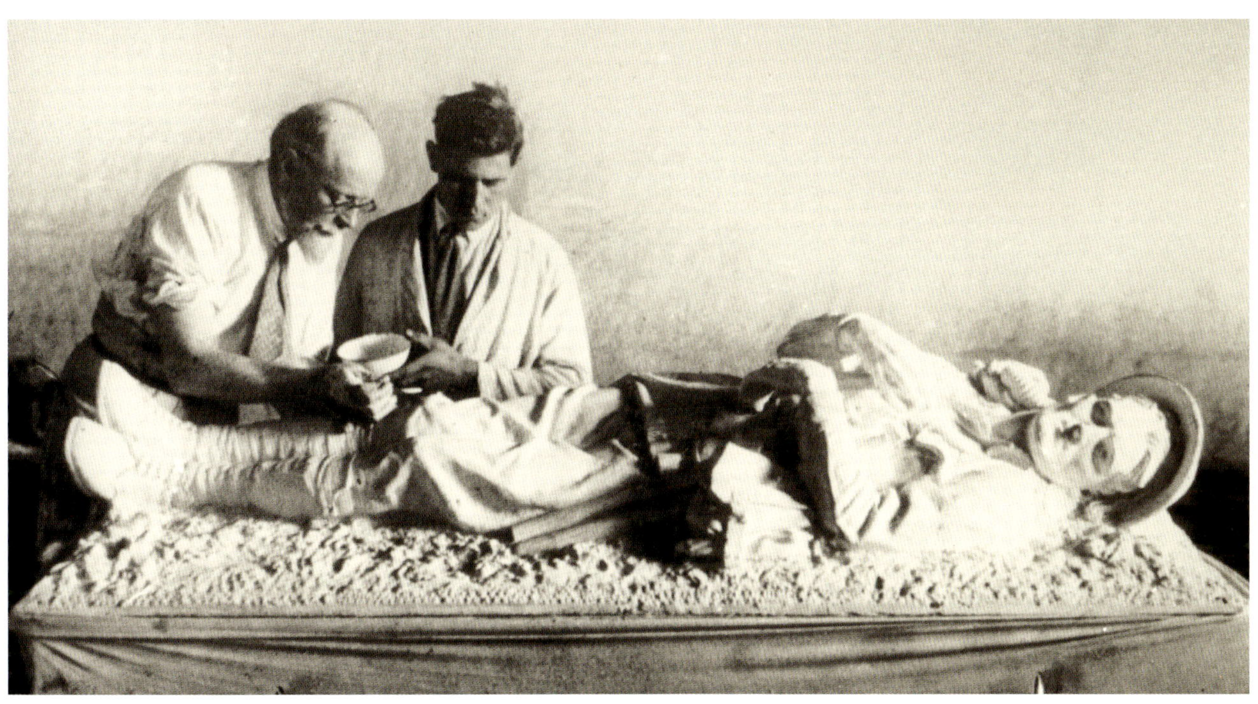

George Lambert and Arthur Murch at Work on the Sculpture 'Recumbent Warrior' 1920
nla.cat-vn464348

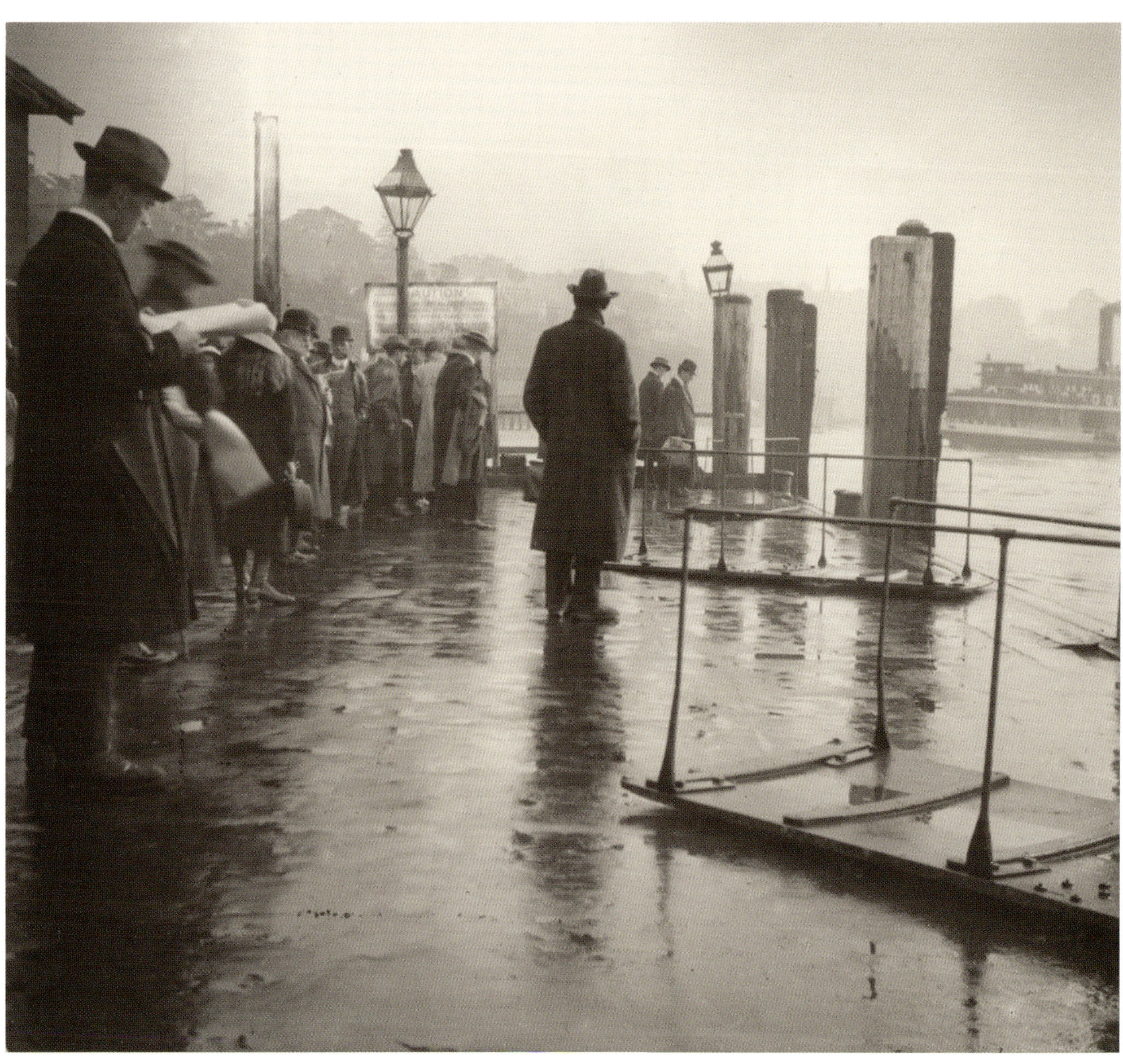

McMahons Point Ferry, Lavender Bay 1909
nla.cat-vn1966092

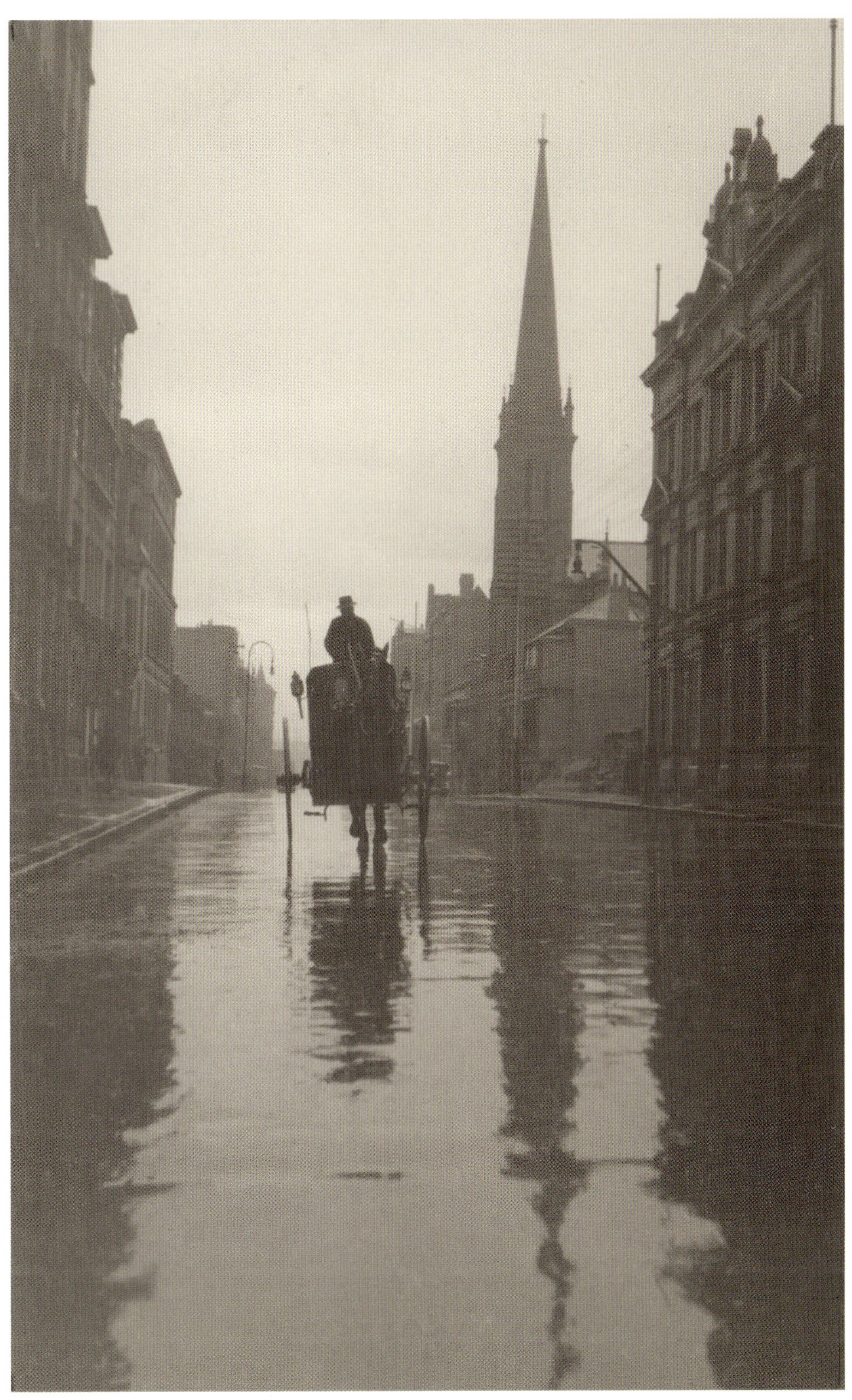

Wet Day, Phillip Street, Sydney c.1910s
nla.cat-vn1965958

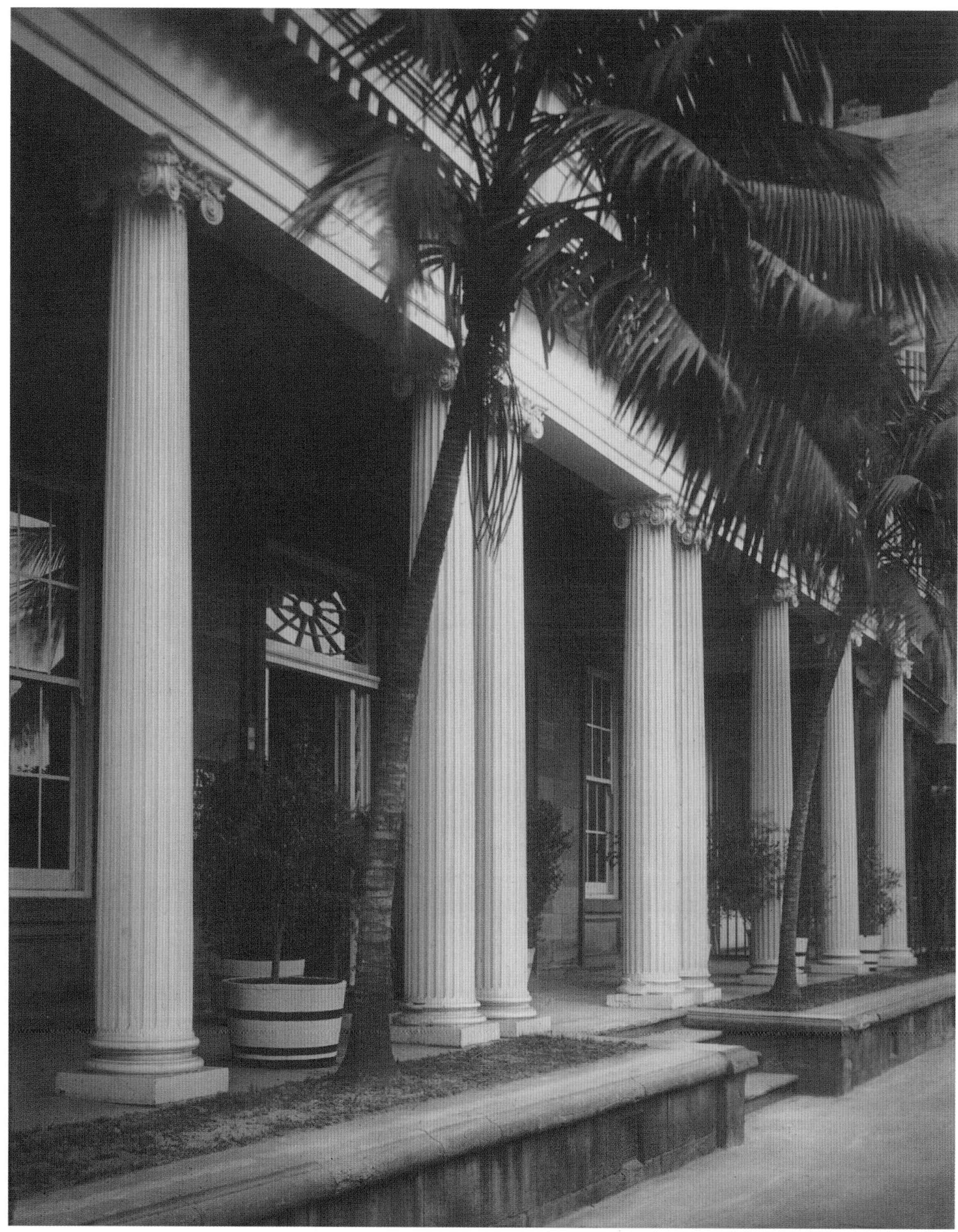

Burdekin House, Macquarie Street, Sydney 1929
nla.cat-vn463357

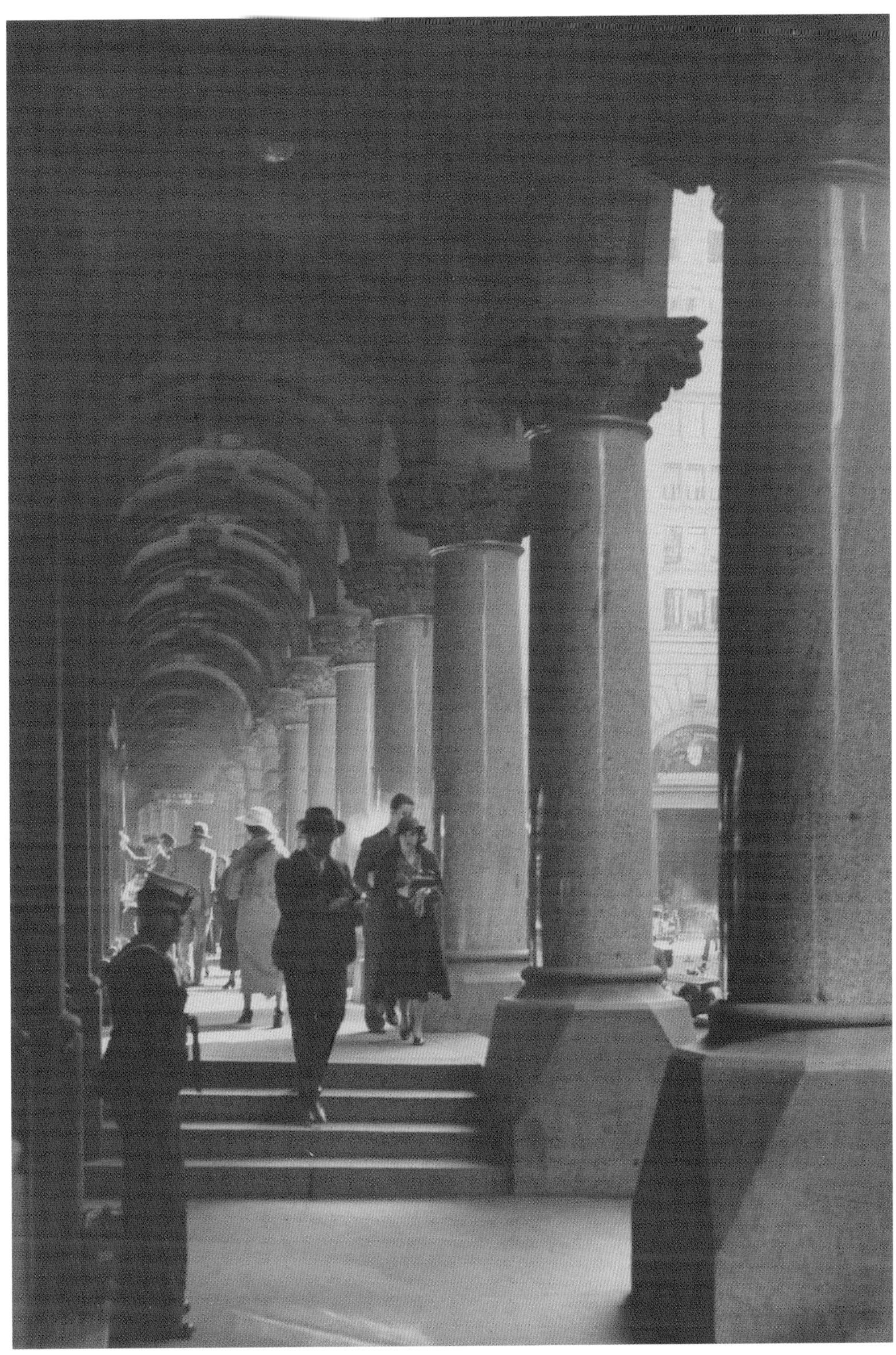

Mail Time, G.P.O., Sydney c.1932
nla.cat-vn464693

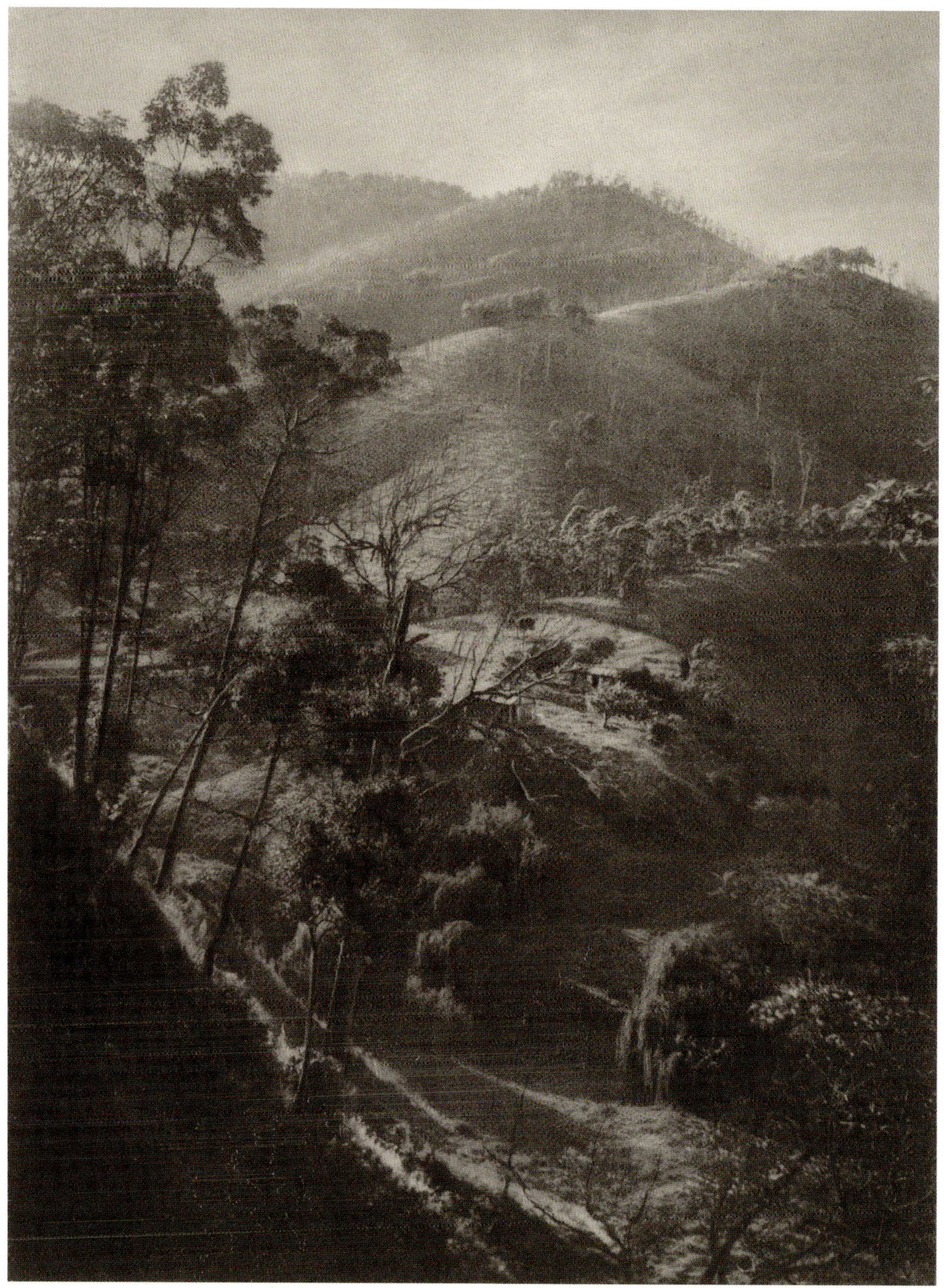

The Ridge, Macleay Valley, New South Wales 1934
nla.cat-vn464959

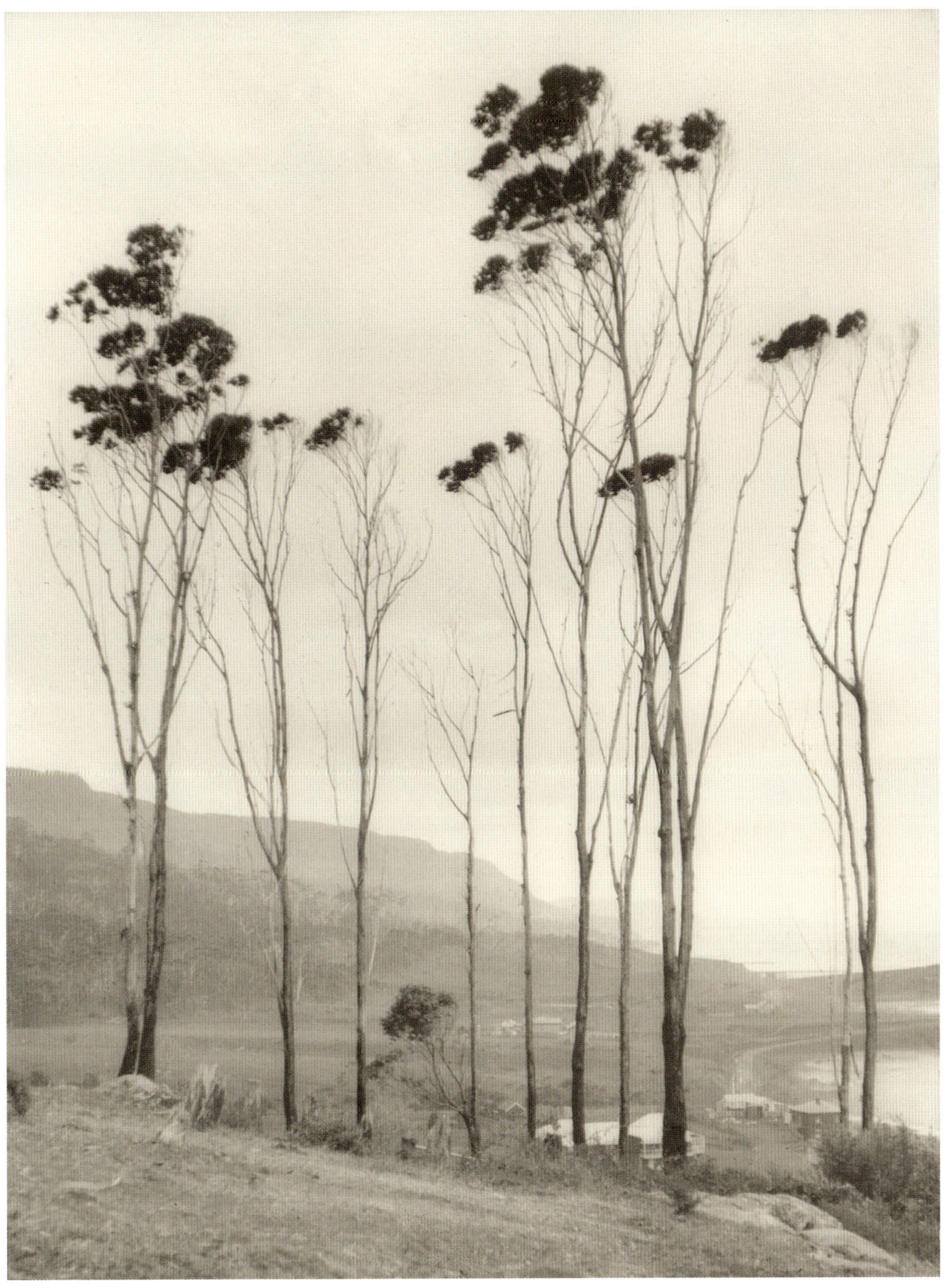

The Sapling Family, Thirroul, New South Wales c.1920s
nla.cat-vn465102

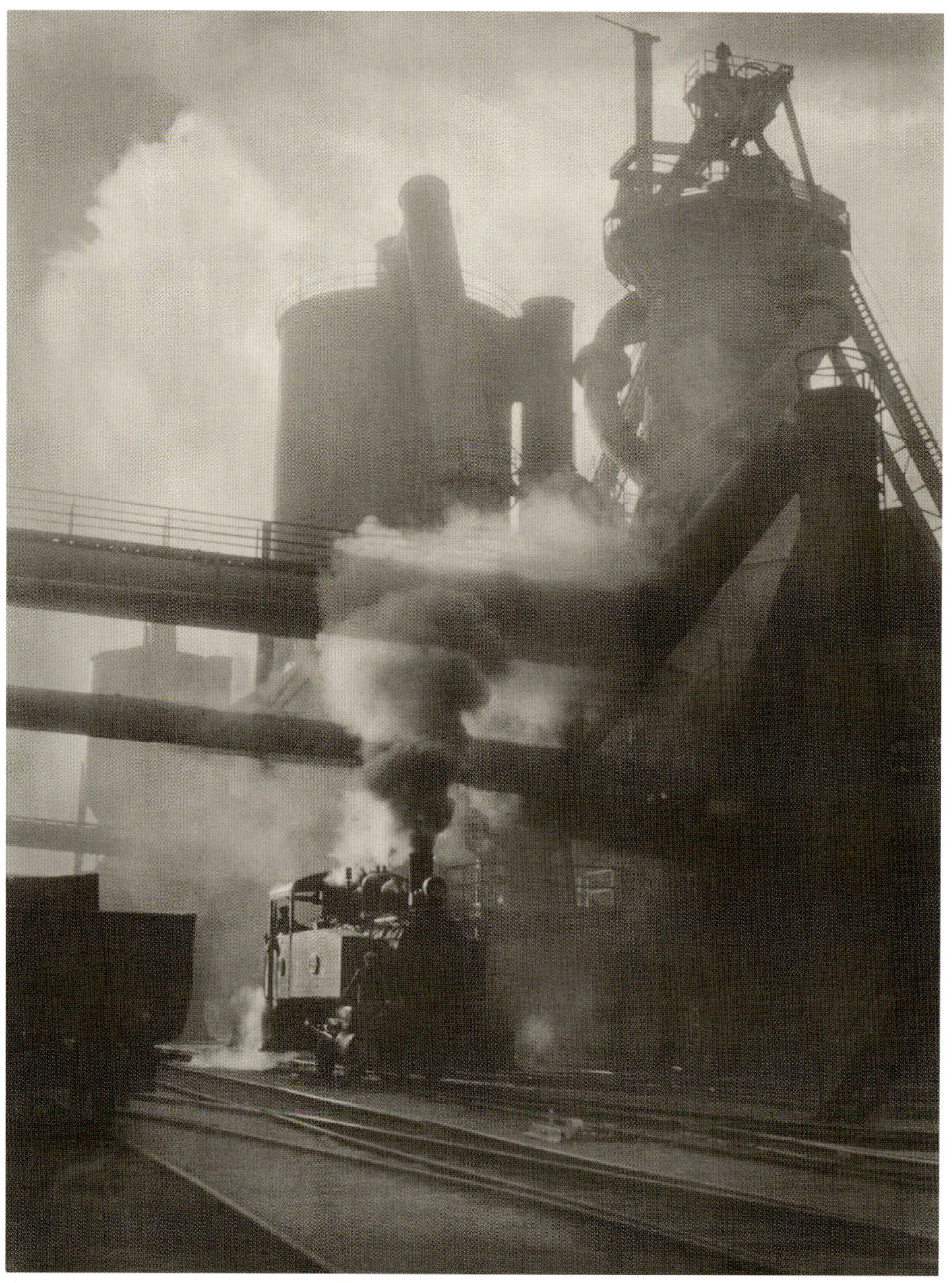

Steam and Sunshine 1934
nla.cat-vn461631

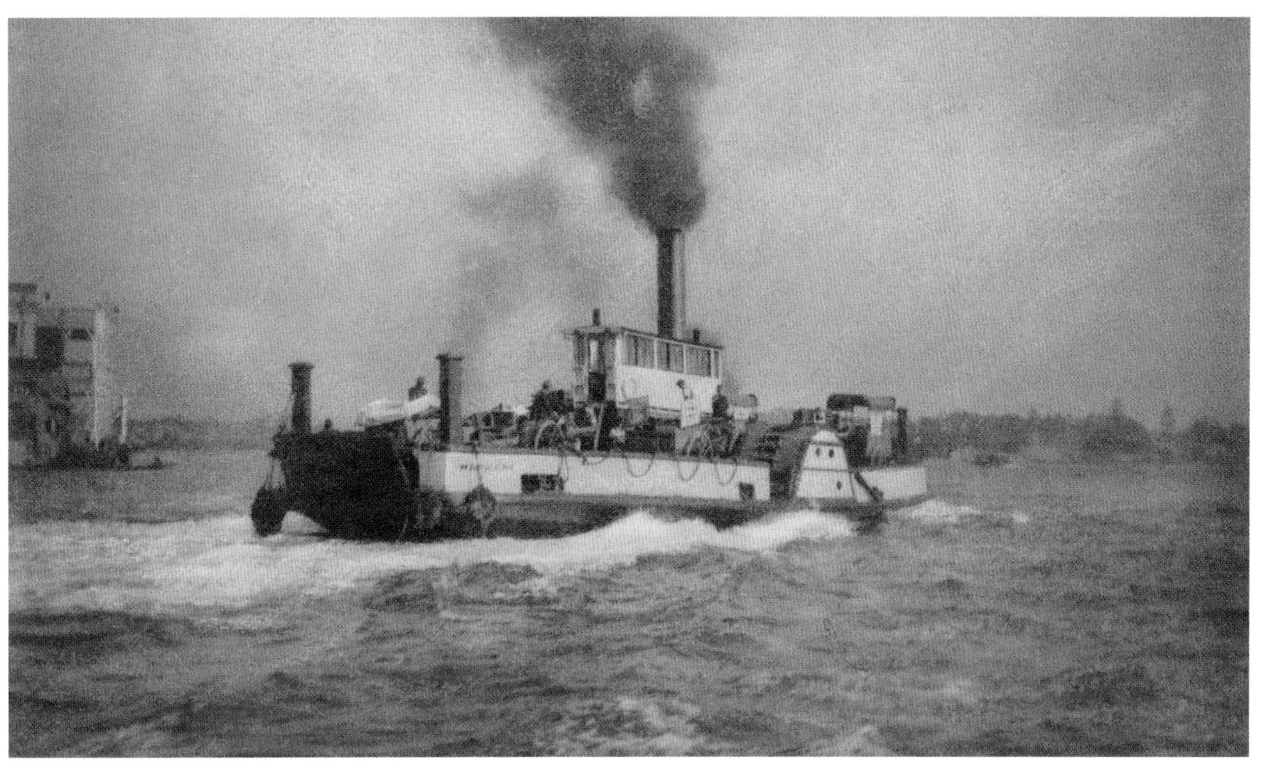

Old Horse Punt, Sydney Harbour, NSW c.1920
nla.cat-vn1963376

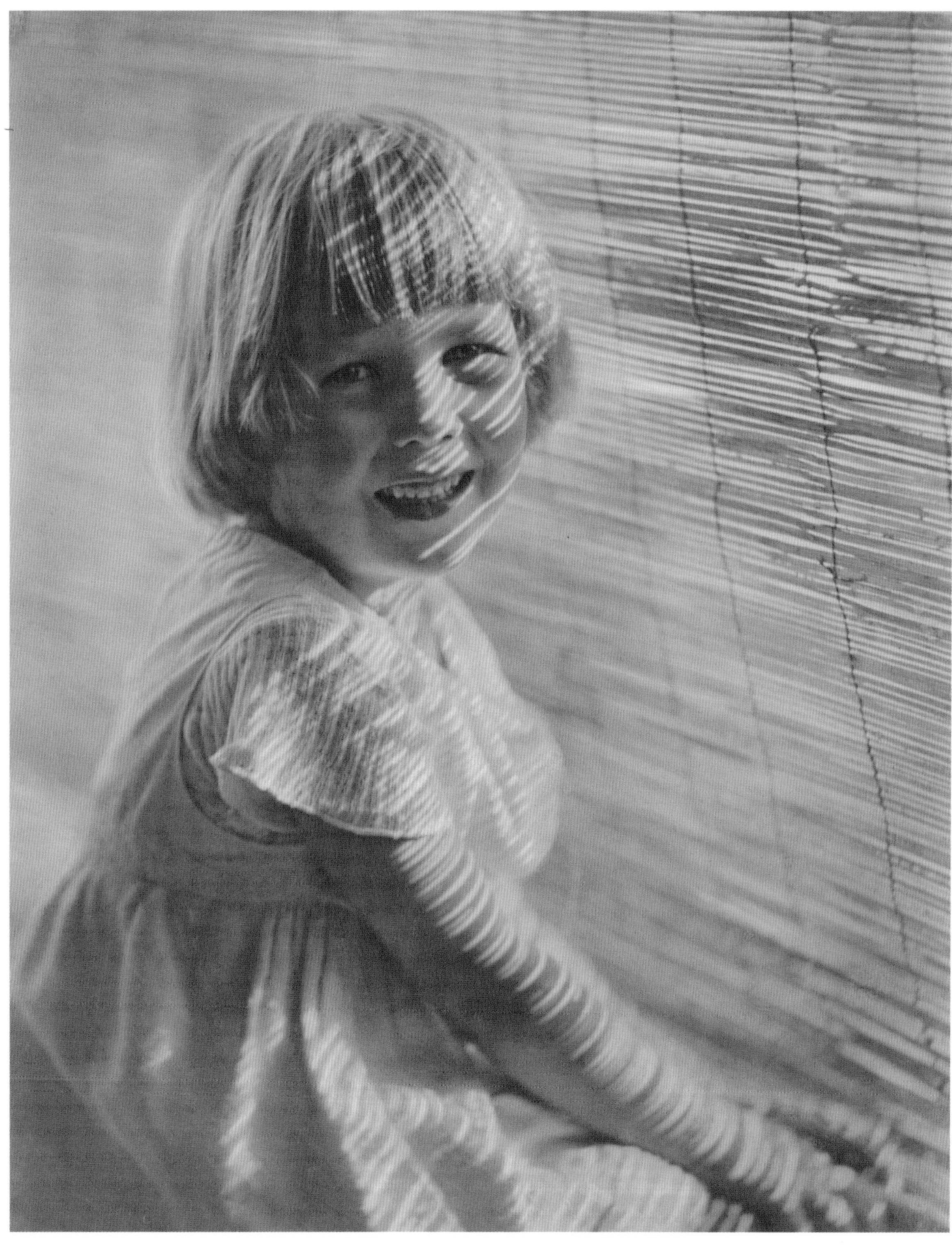

The Bamboo Blind: Portrait of Beryl Cazneaux c.1915
nla.cat-vn463777

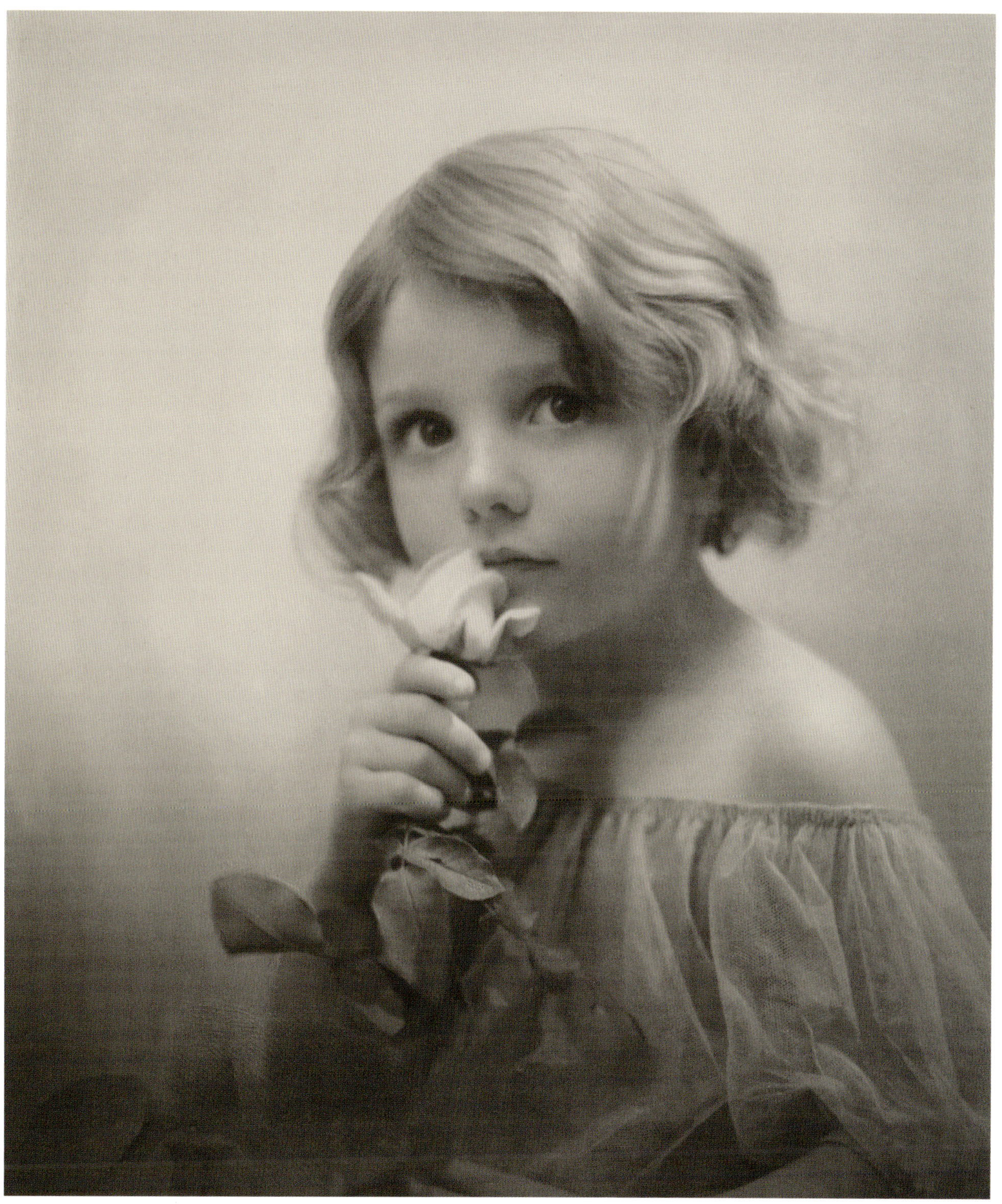

The Child, the Blossom, Angela: Portrait of Lorne Campbell c.1934
nla.cat-vn463792

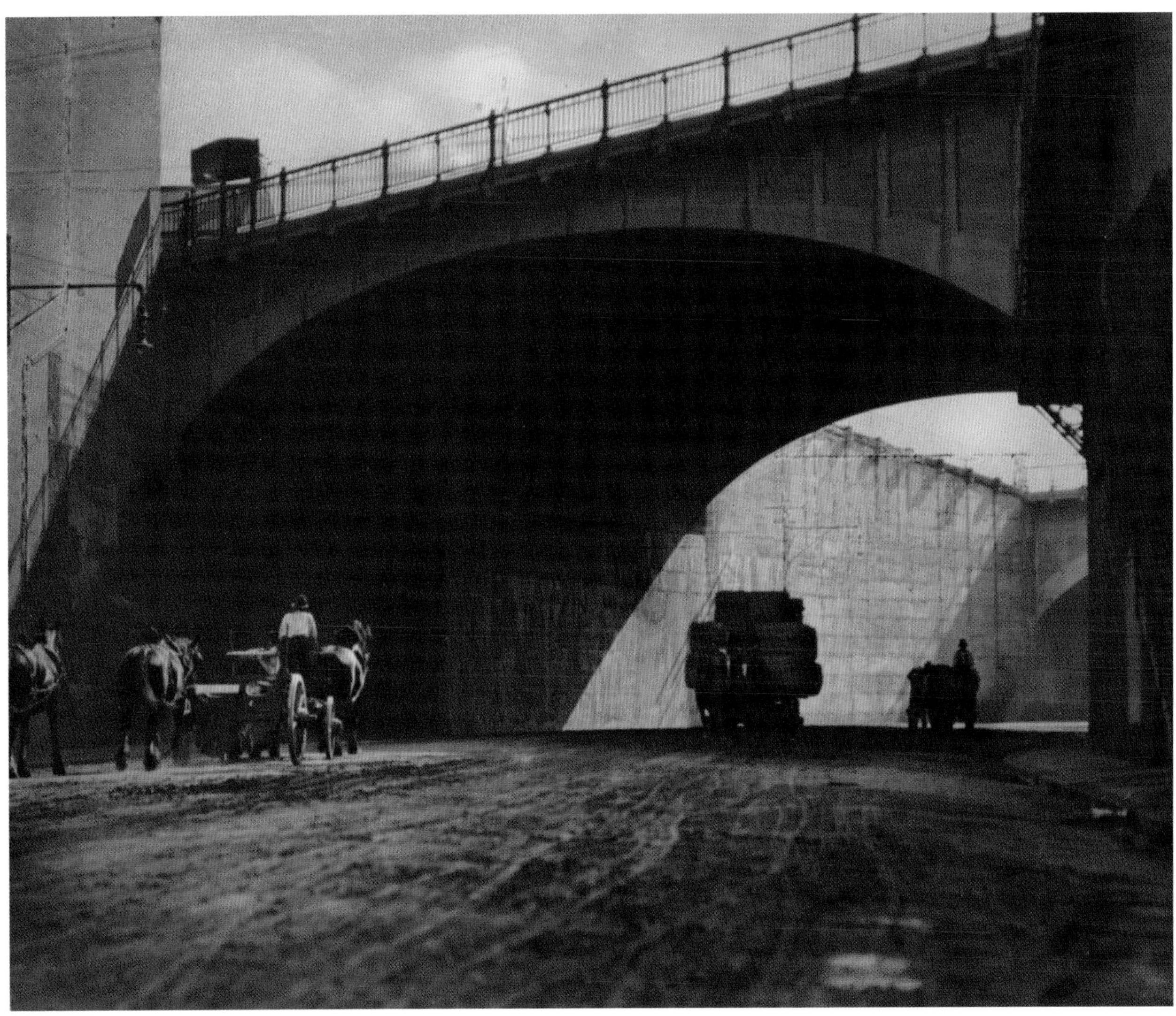

The Wharf Road, Sydney c.1918
nla.cat-vn464590

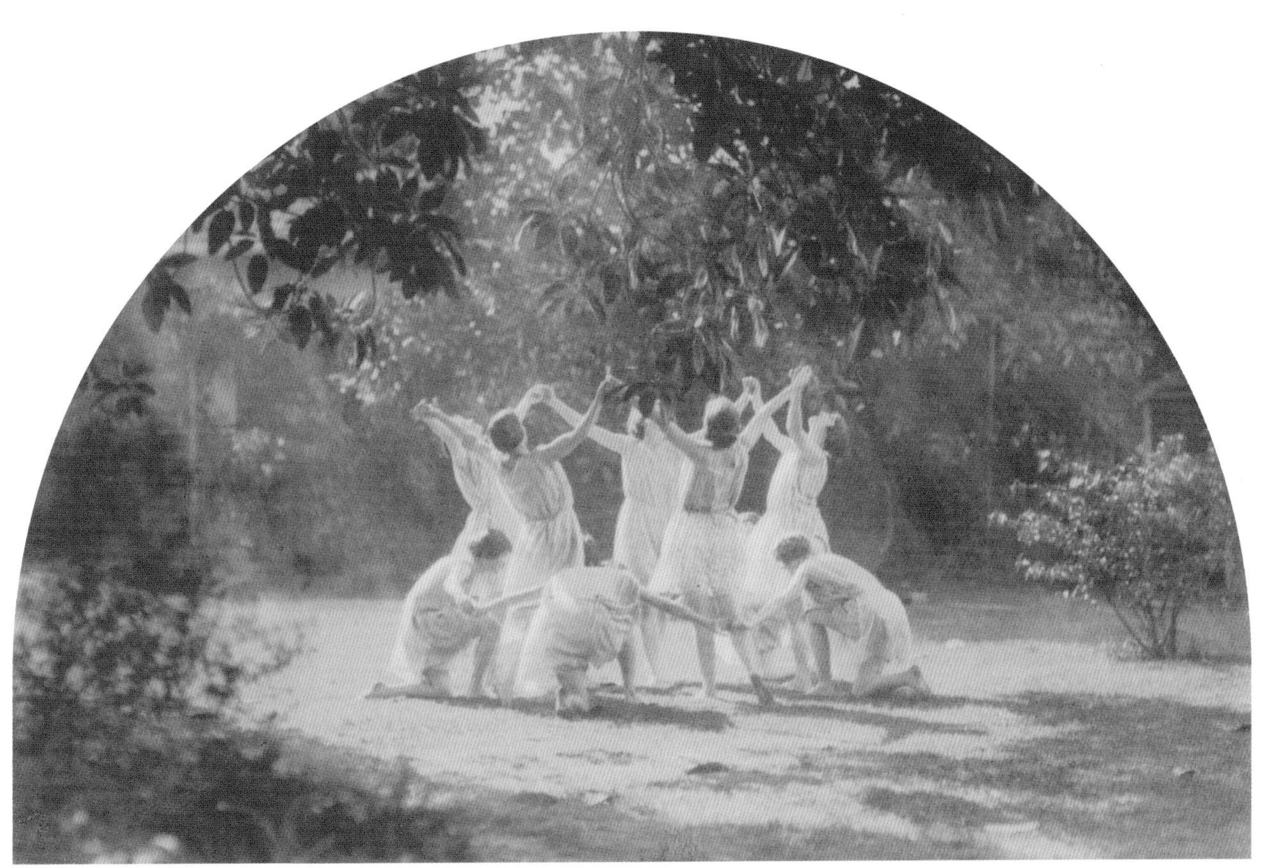

Grecian Dance 1924
nla.cat-vn464197

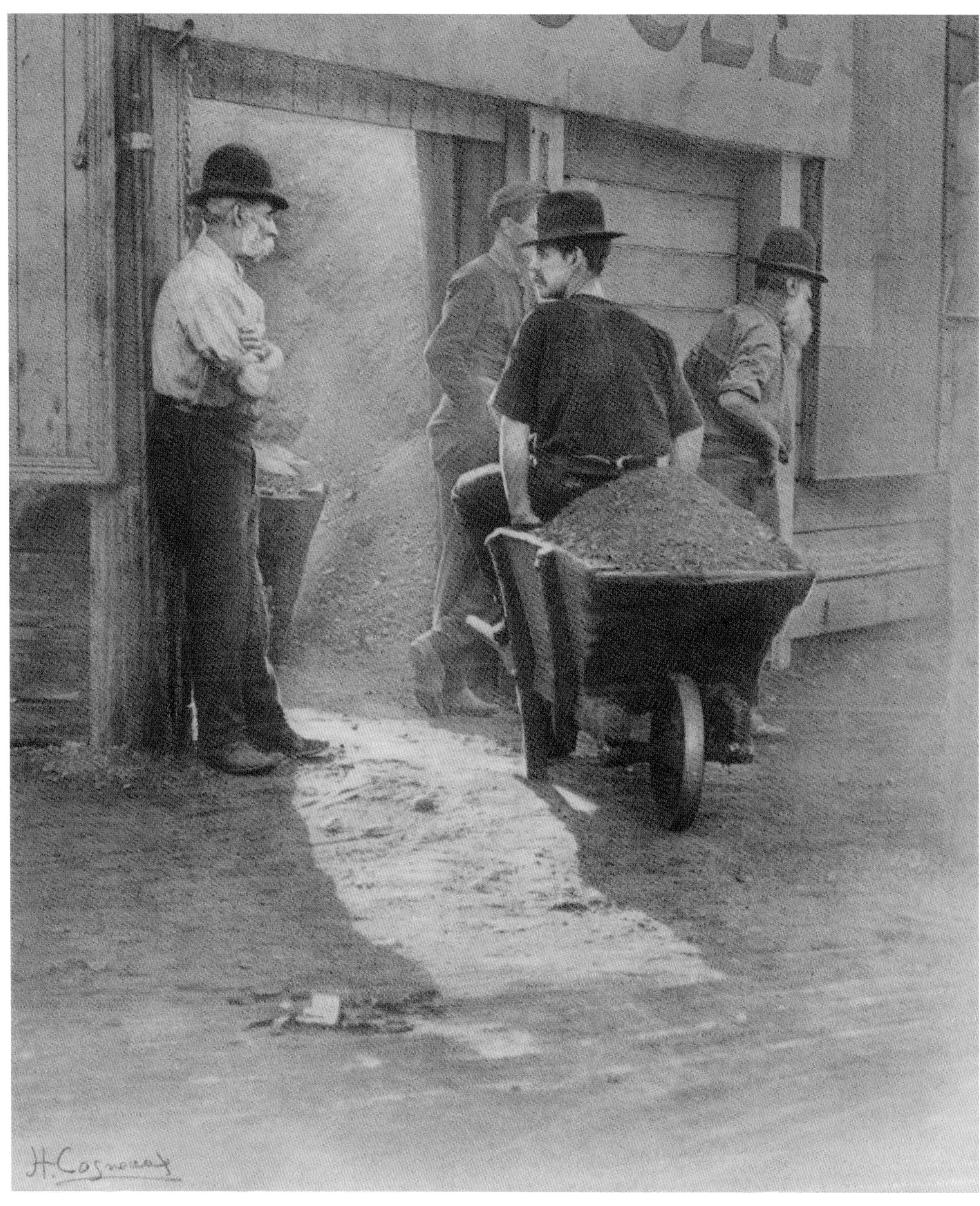

Old Coal Depot, Milson's Point 1907
nla.cat-vn1987089

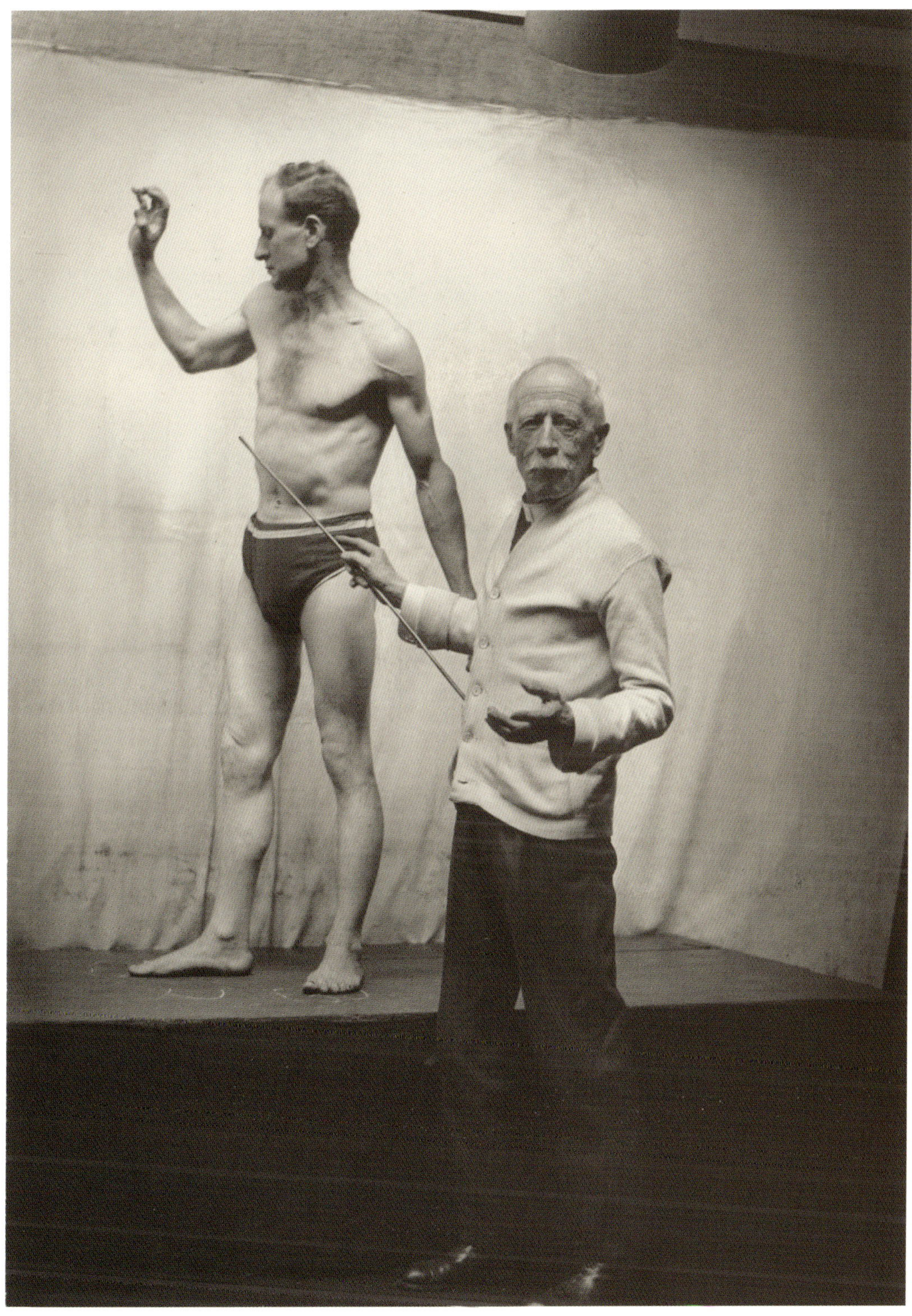

Julian Ashton, the Art Class c.1920
nla.cat-vn1986839

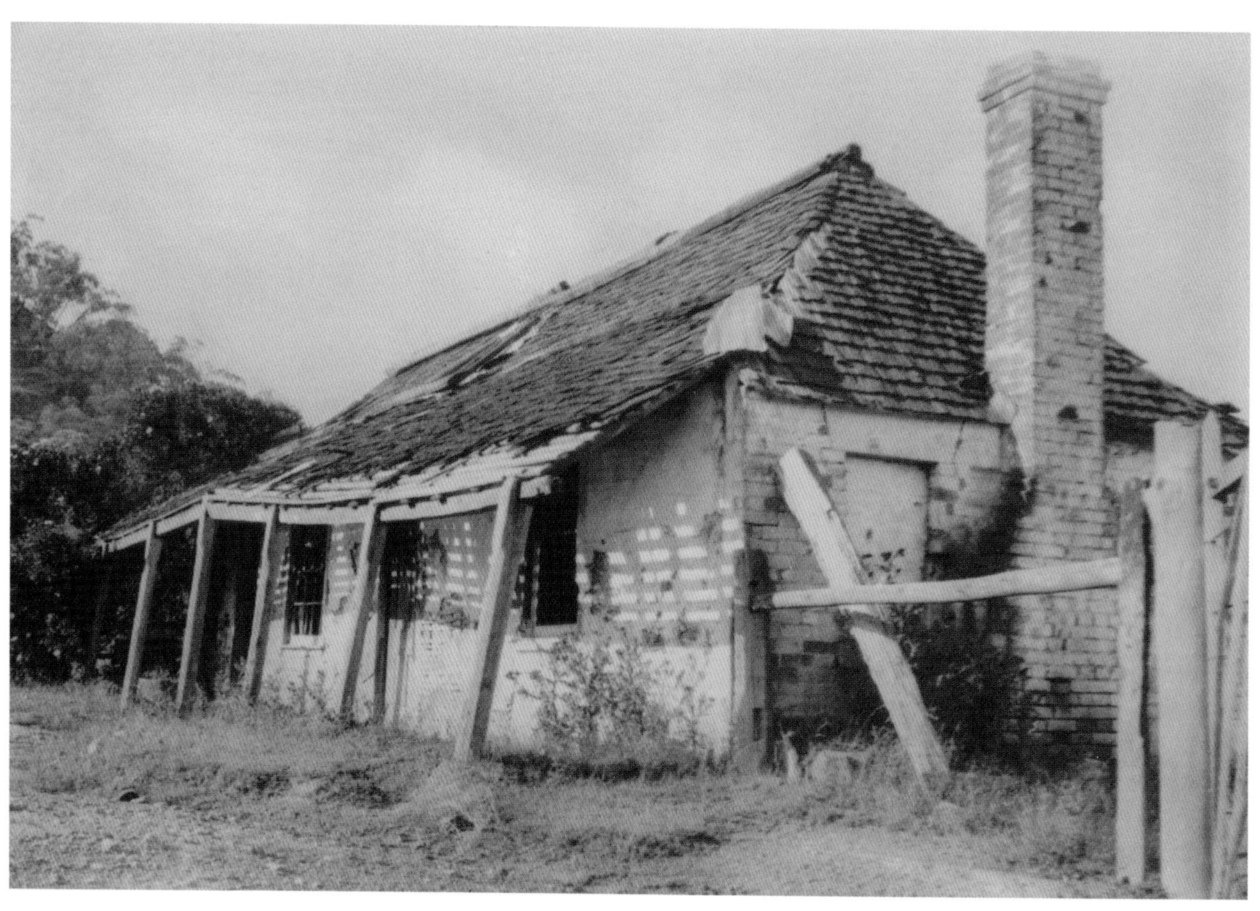

Old Cottage, Little Hartley, New South Wales between 1920 and 1929
nla.cat-vn1987098

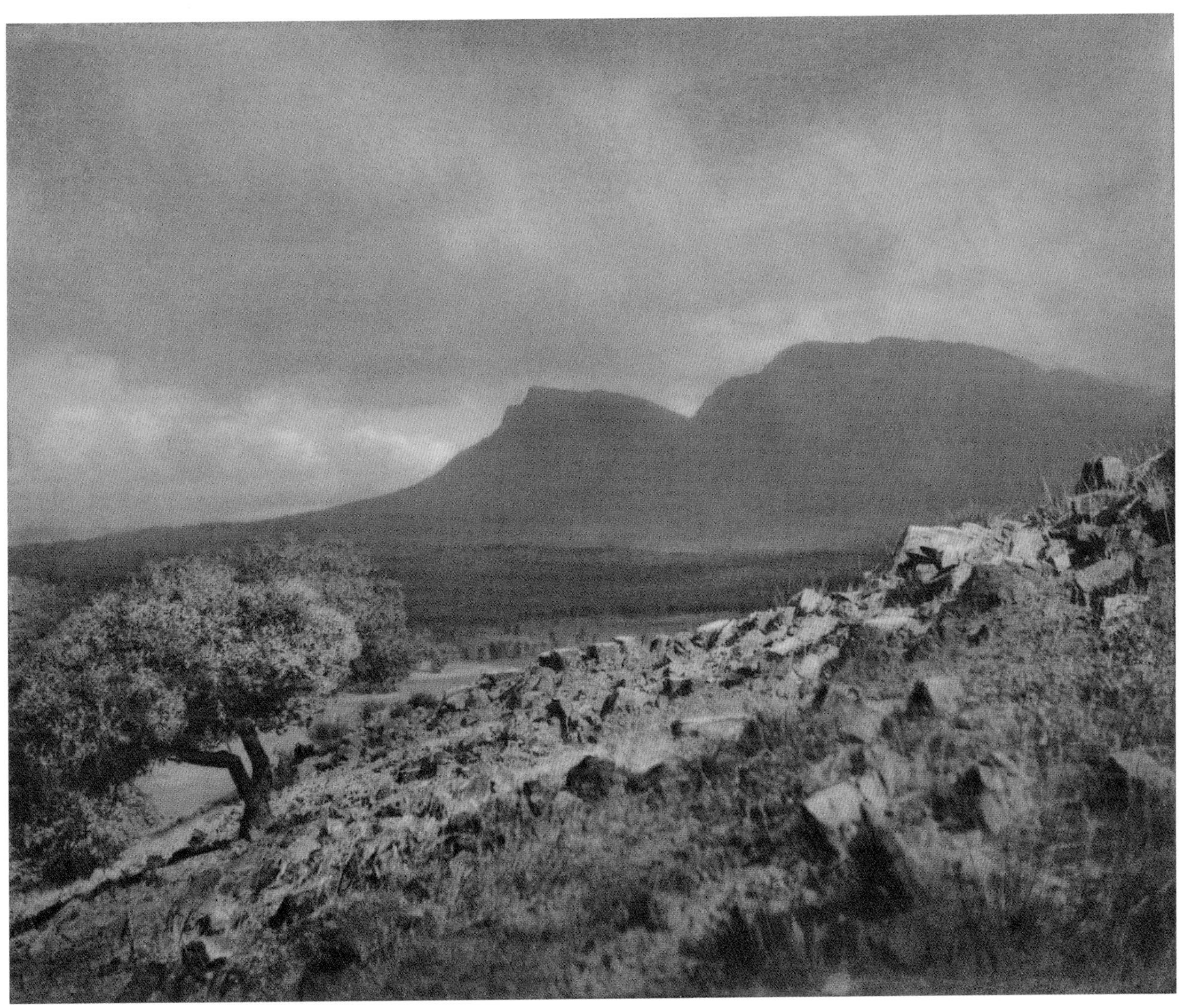

Profile of the Flinders, Wilpena Pound, Flinders Range, South Australia c.1937
nla.cat-vn464900

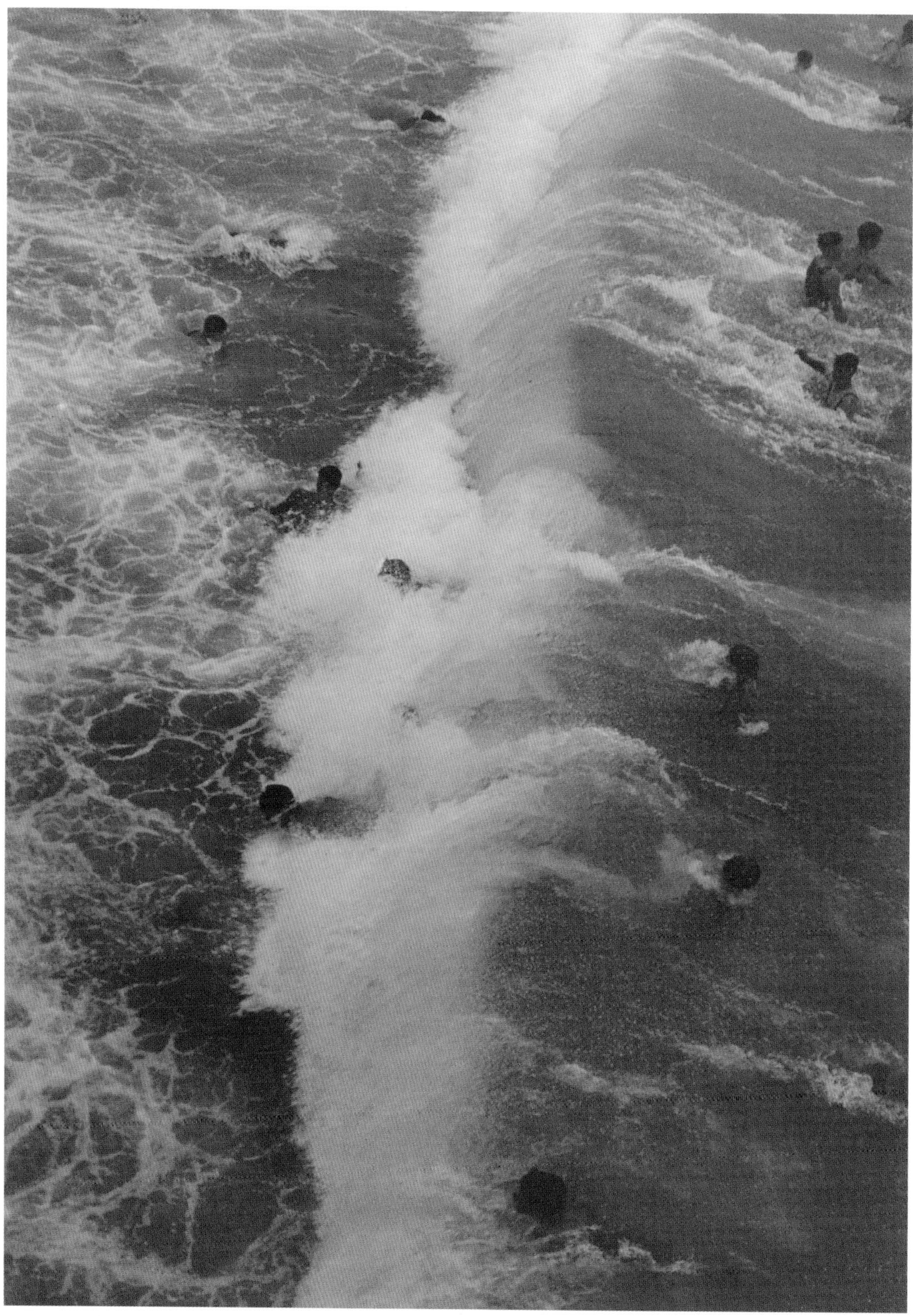

Sydney Surfing 1929
nla.cat-vn1984090

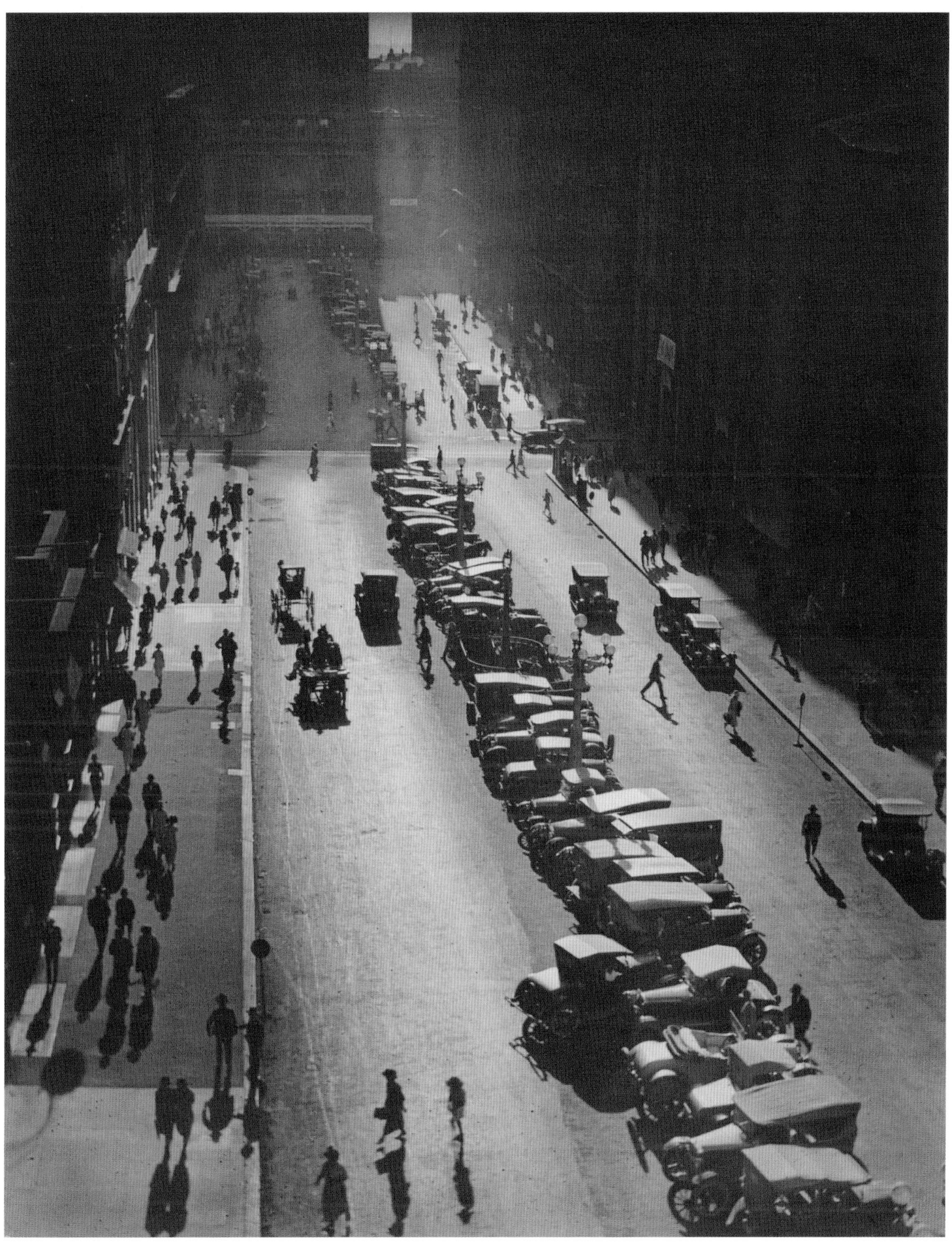

Martin Place 1925
nla.cat-vn1987117

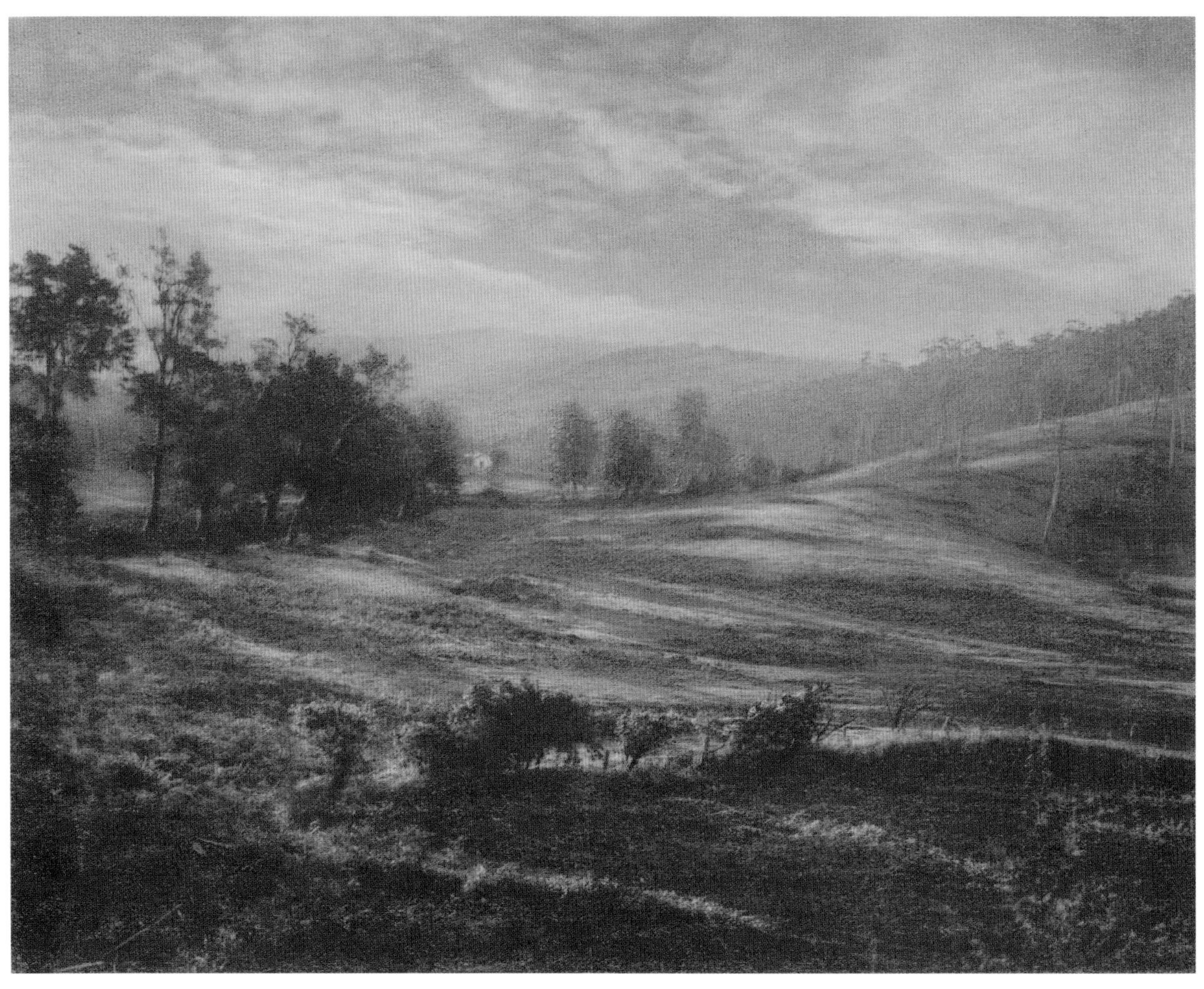

A Settler's Home, New South Wales c.1935
nla.cat-vn1987443

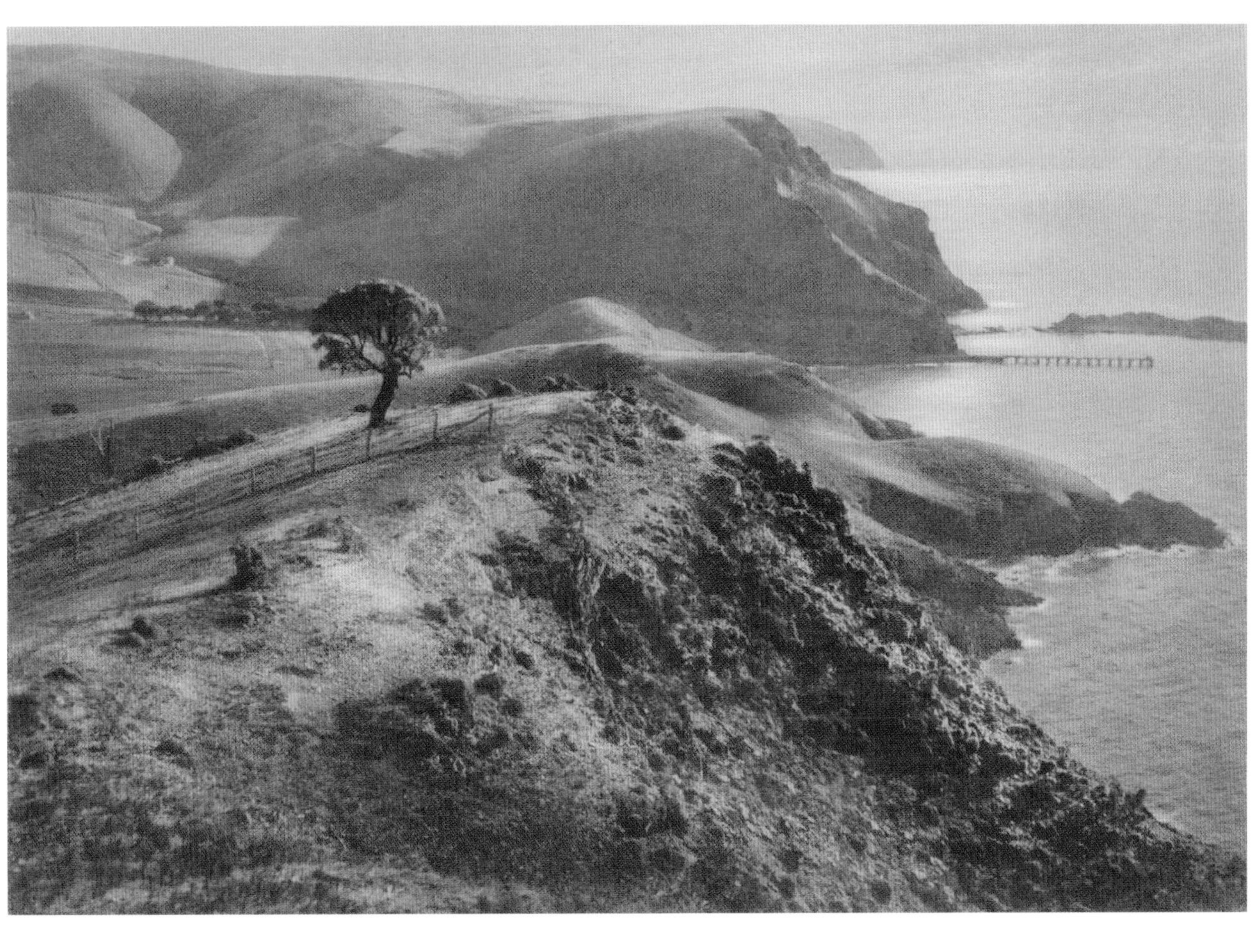

The Valley by the Sea, South Australia 1937
nla.cat-vn1987544

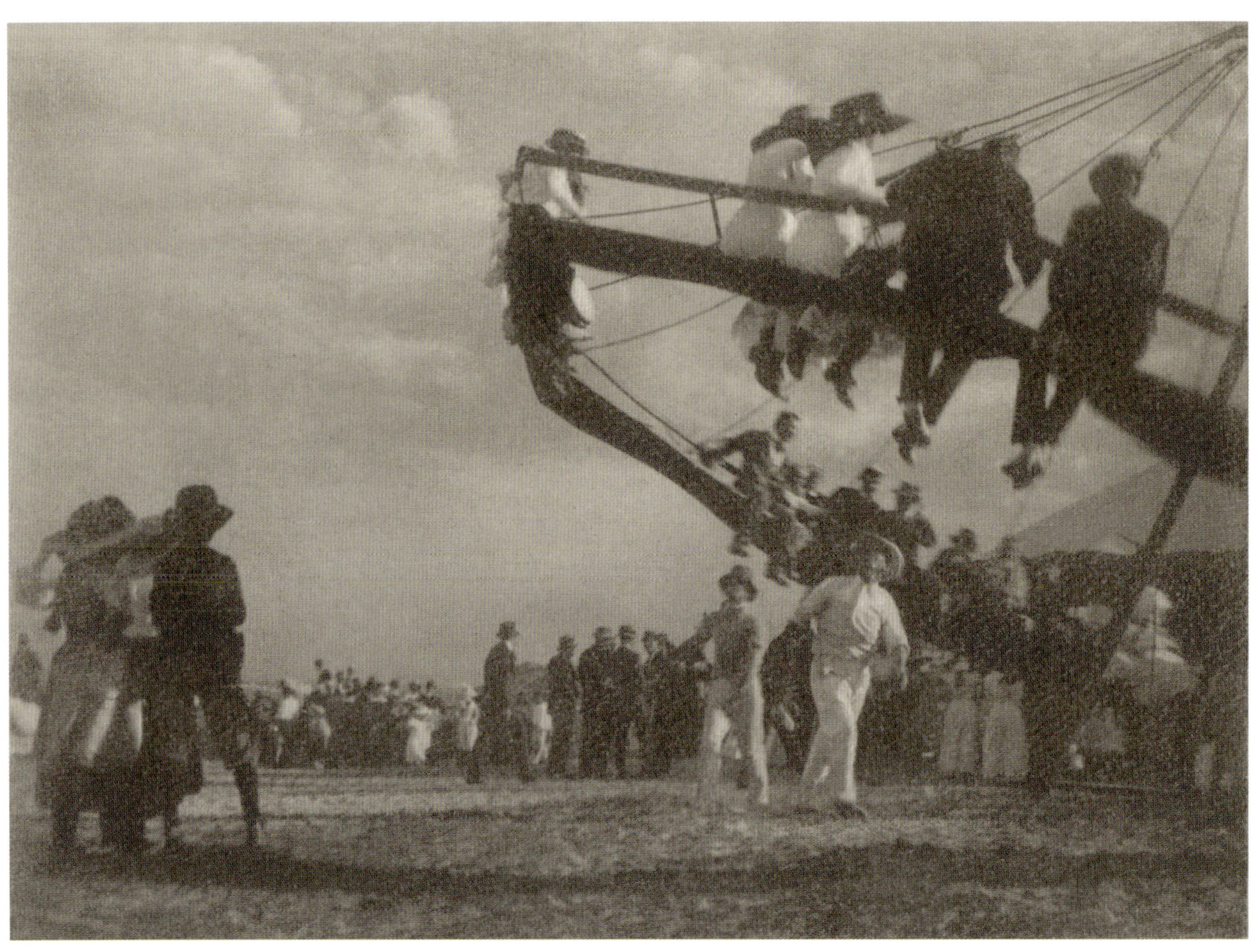

The Razzle Dazzle 1910
nla.cat-vn464374

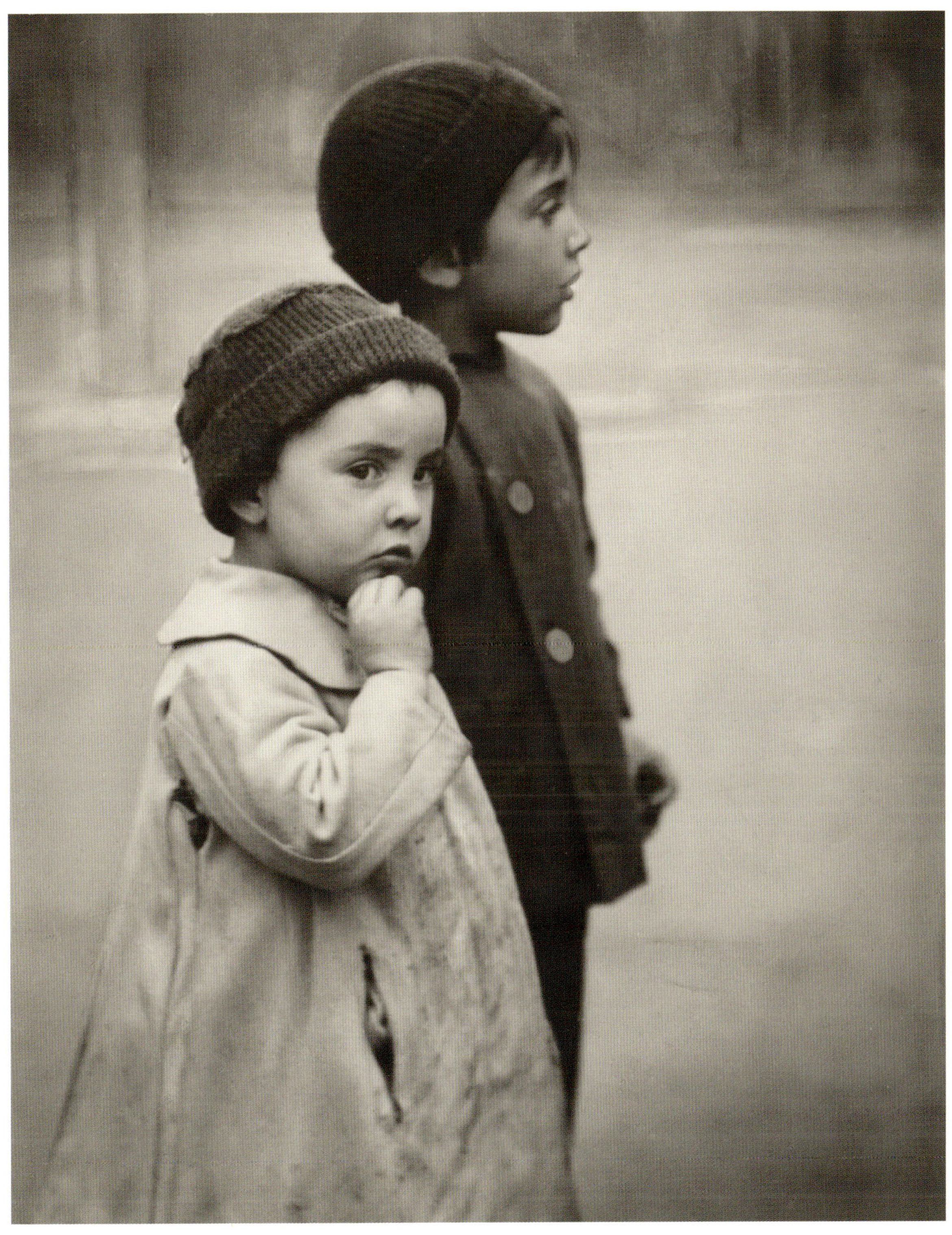

Little Strangers c.1914
nla.cat-vn463756

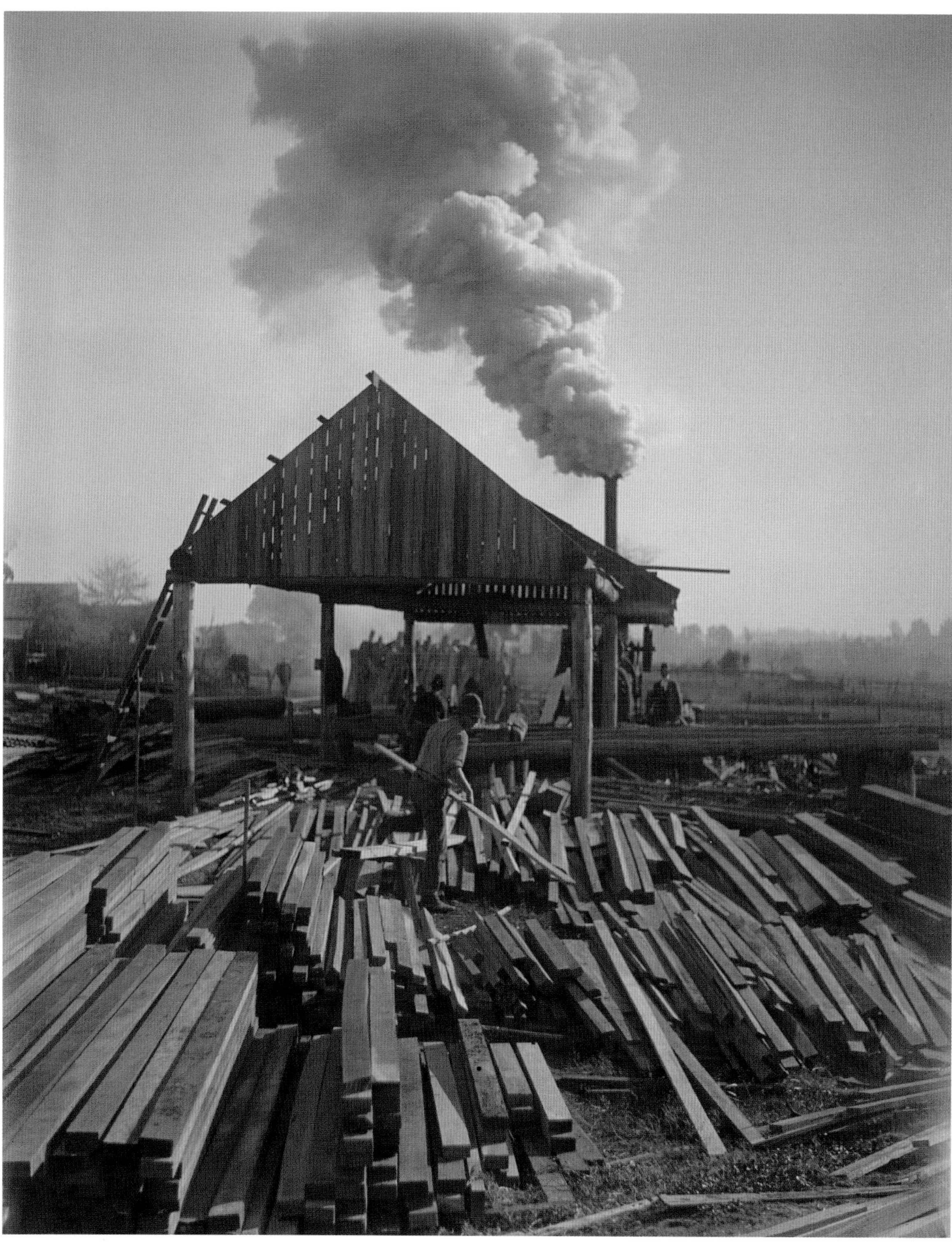

Timber Mill, Camden c.1910
nla.cat-vn3044977

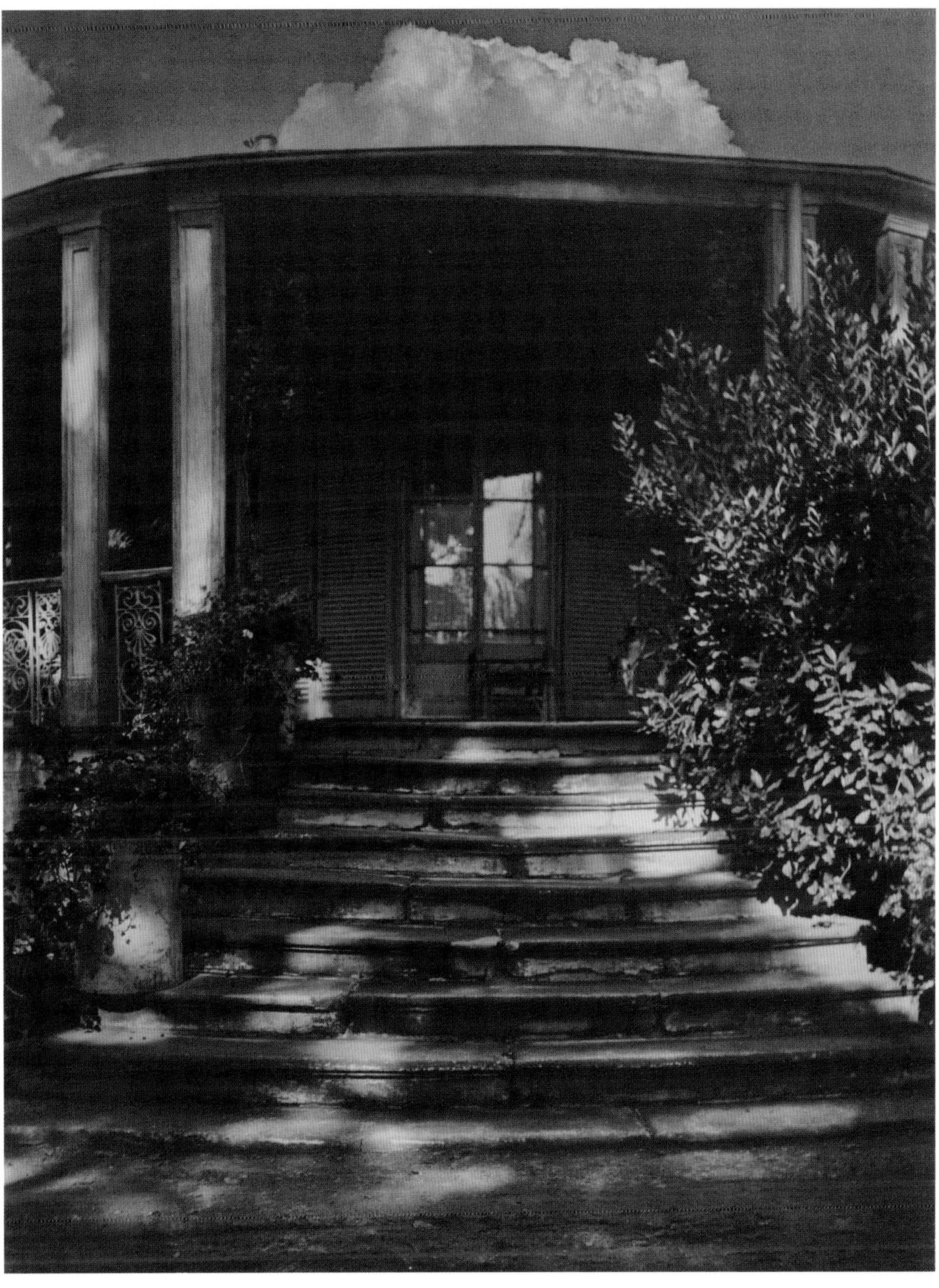

Greystanes: the Cox Home on Prospect Hill 1920
nla.cat-vn1986142

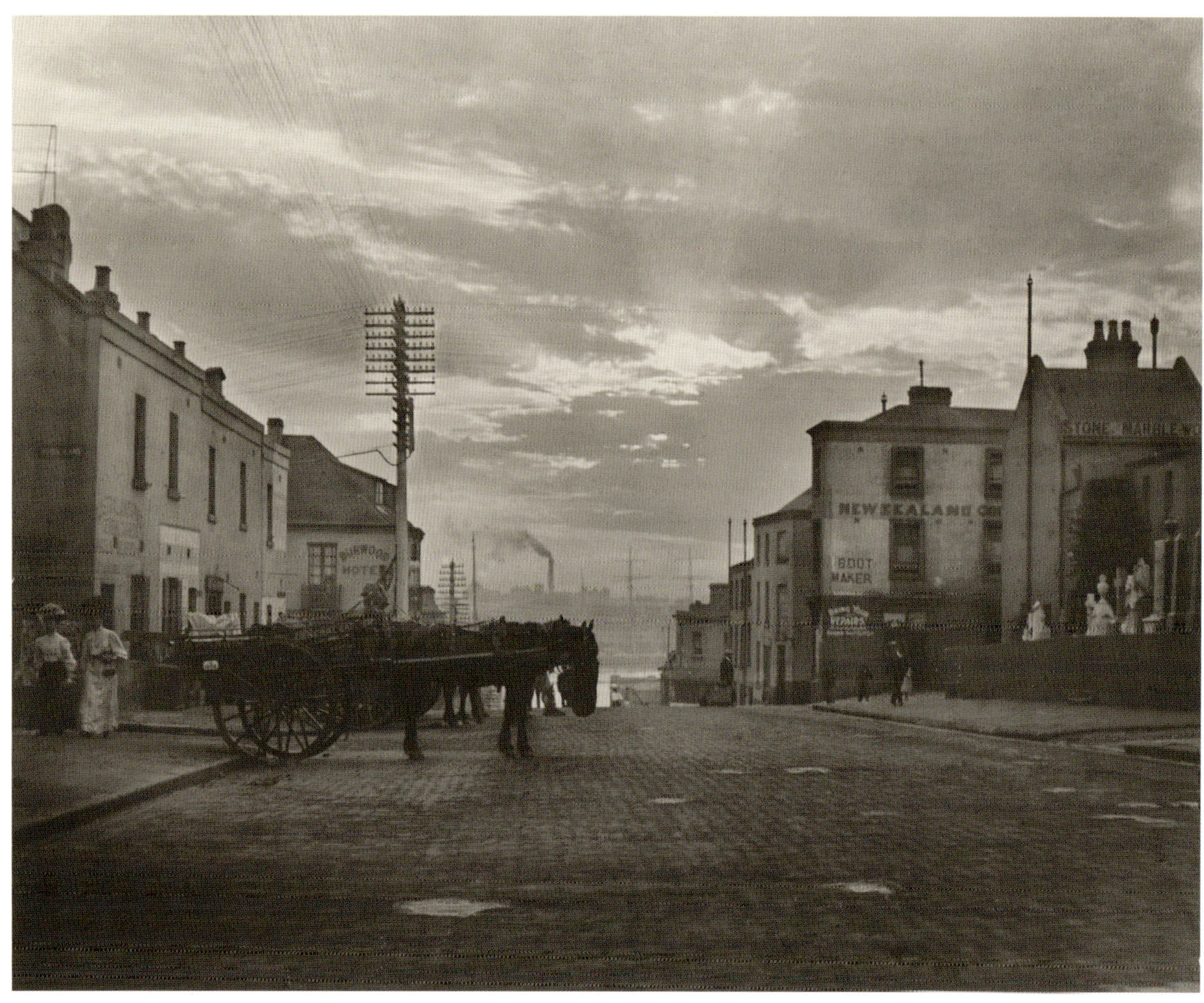

Margaret Street, Sydney, NSW 1908
nla.cat-vn464667

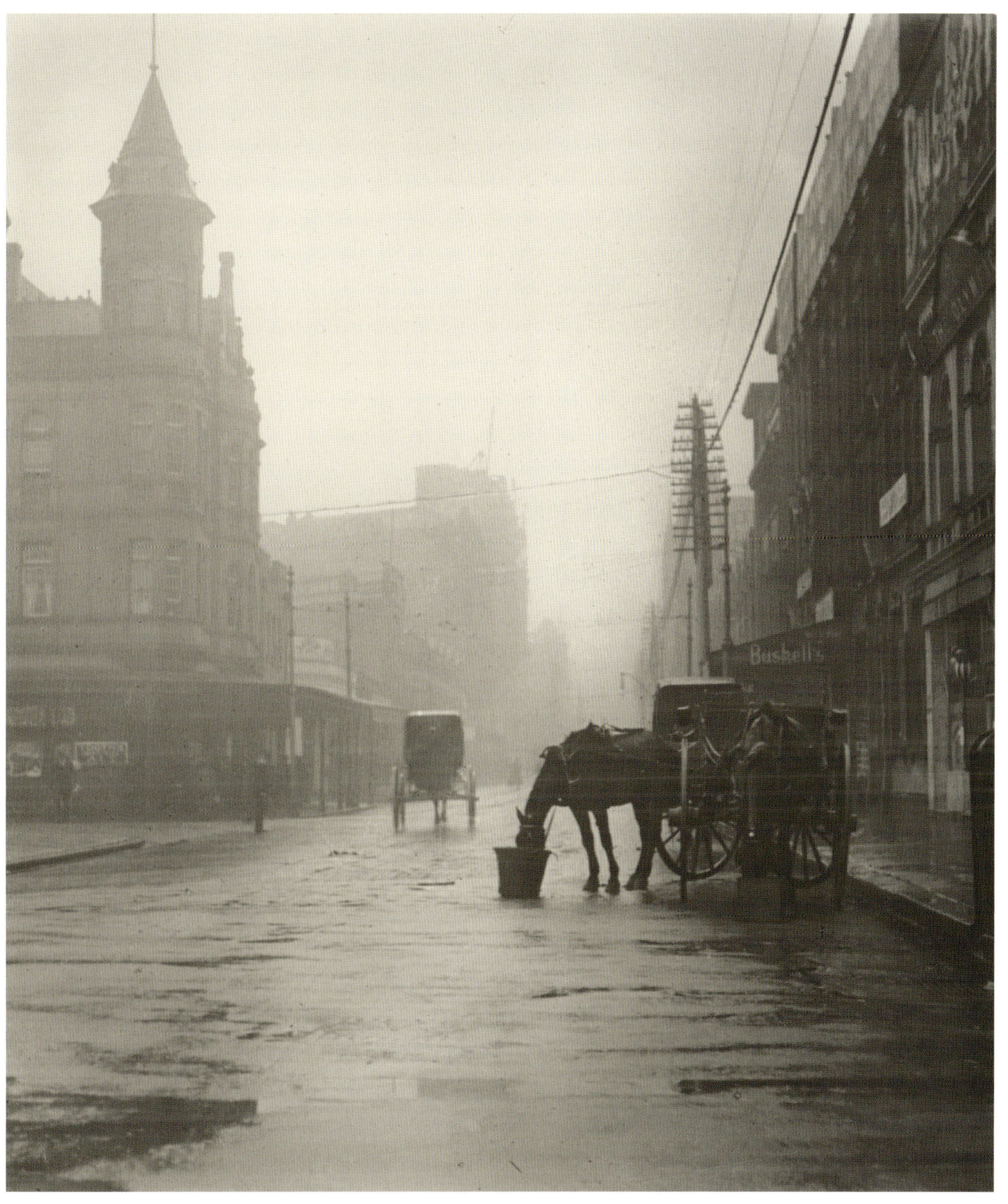

Early Morning, Pitt Street, Sydney 1909
nla.cat-vn464365

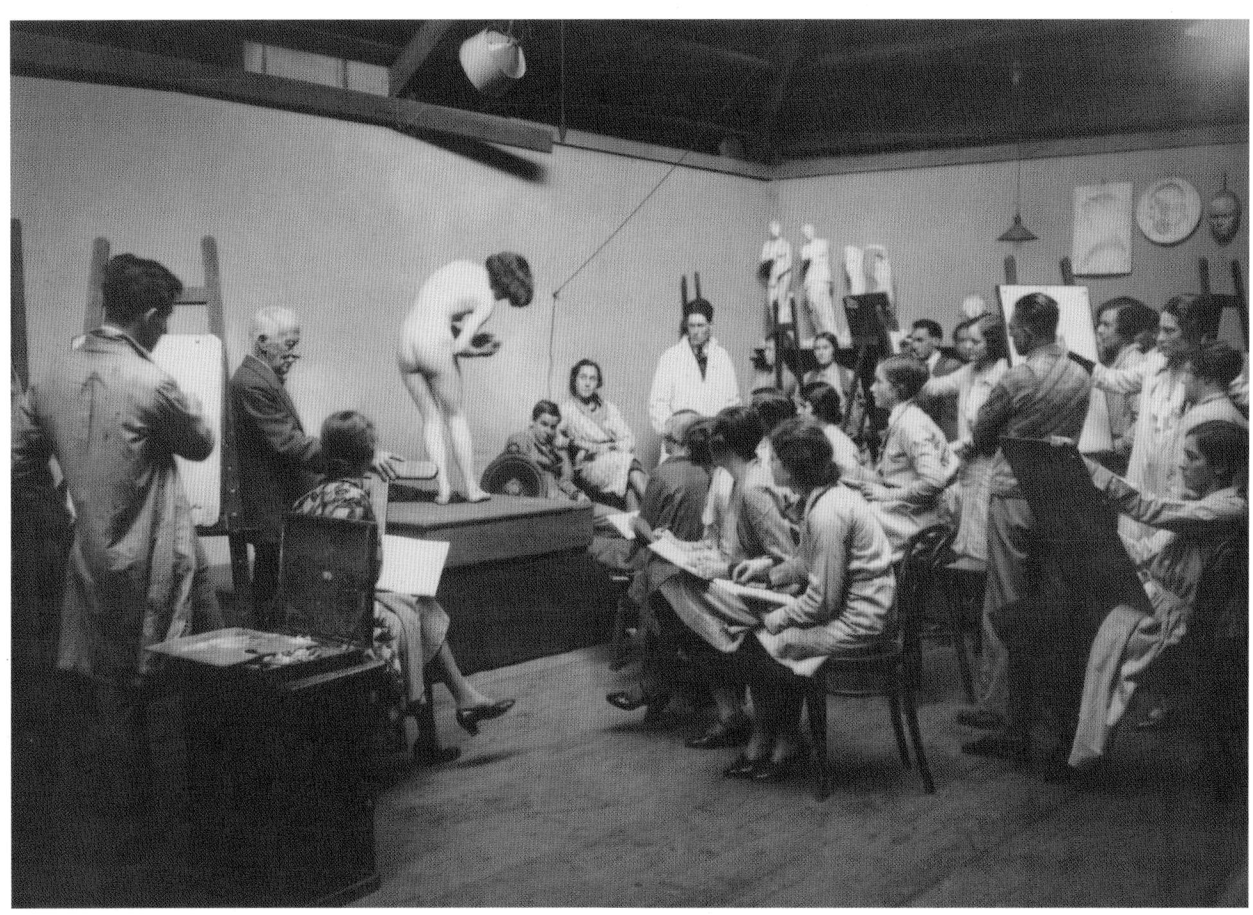

The Life Class 1931
nla.cat-vn1986749

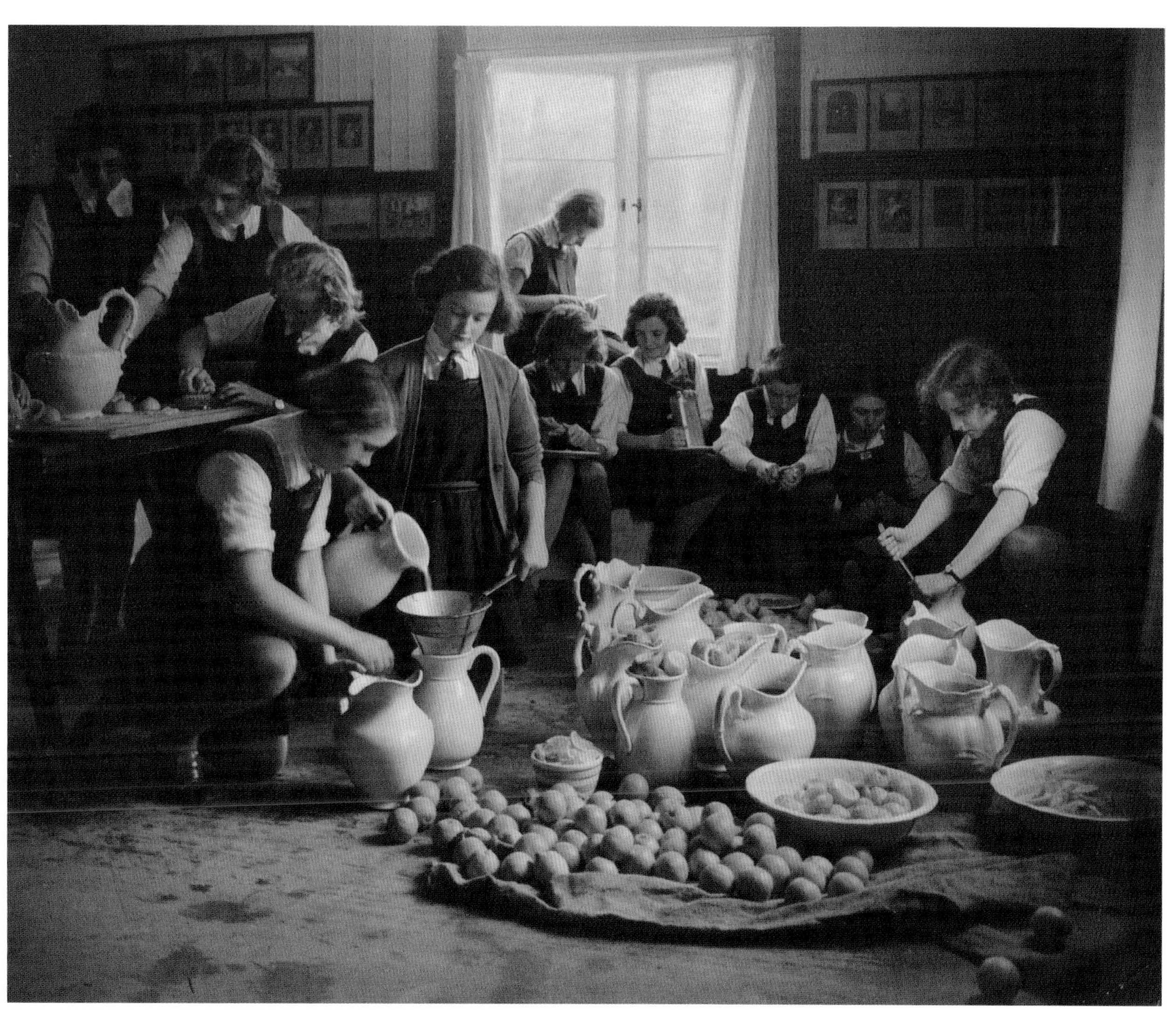

Oranges and Lemons 1934
nla.cat-vn282777

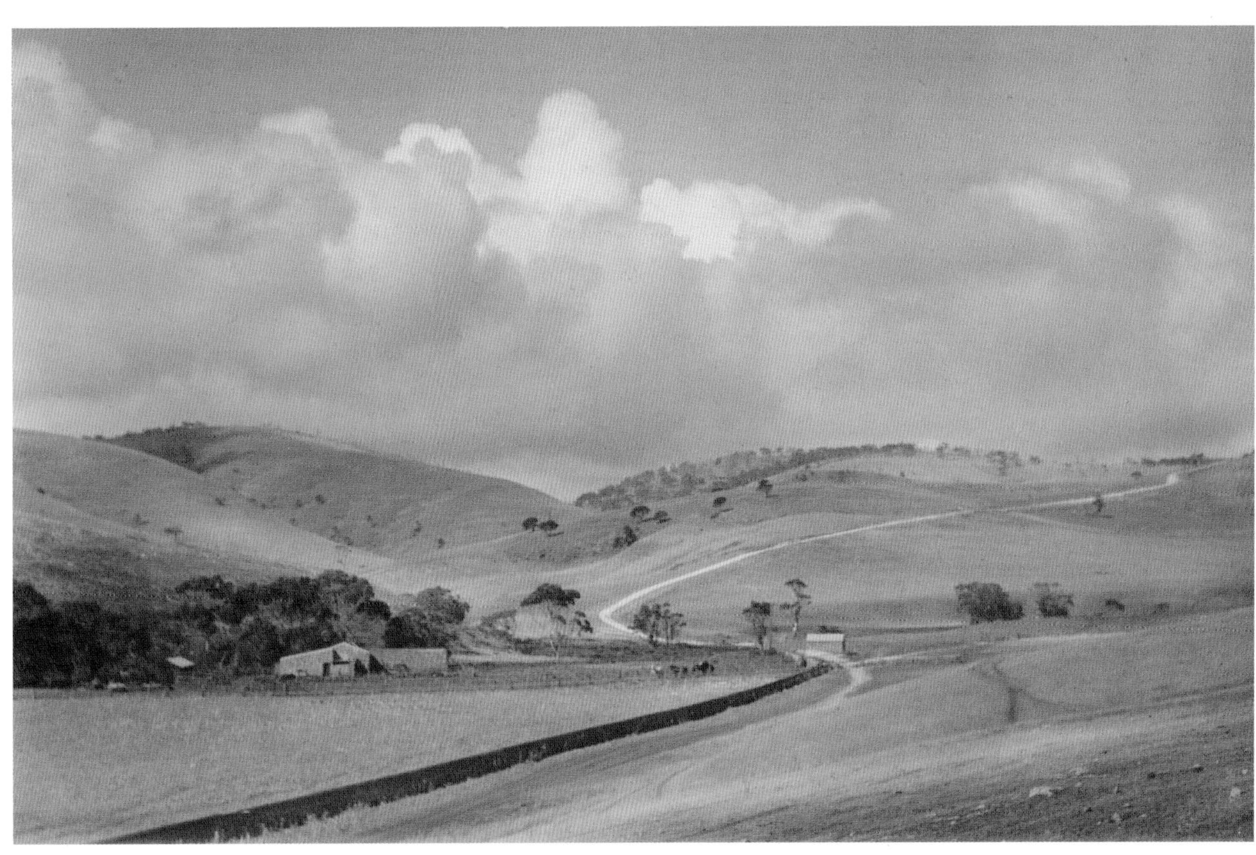

Road up the Hill 1937
nla.cat-vn464950

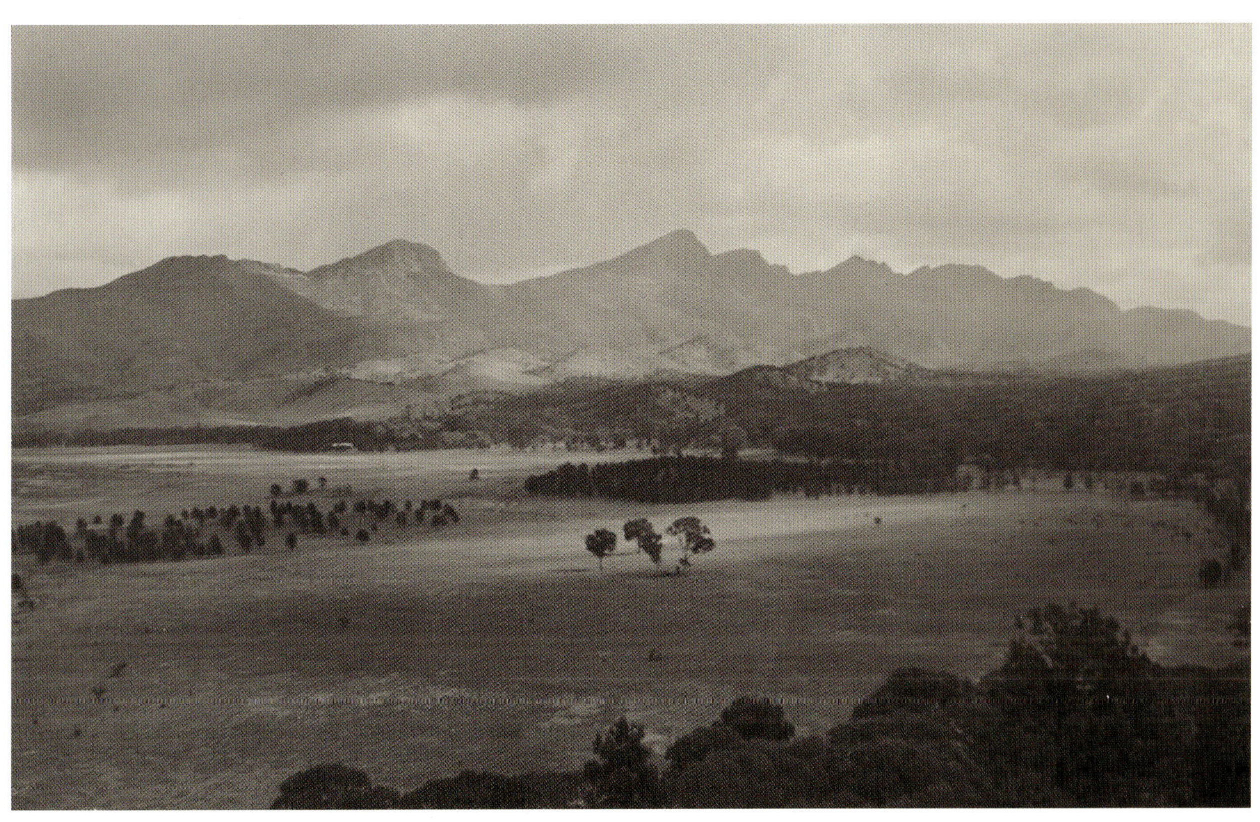

Wilpena Heights, South Australia c.1937
nla.cat-vn1987459

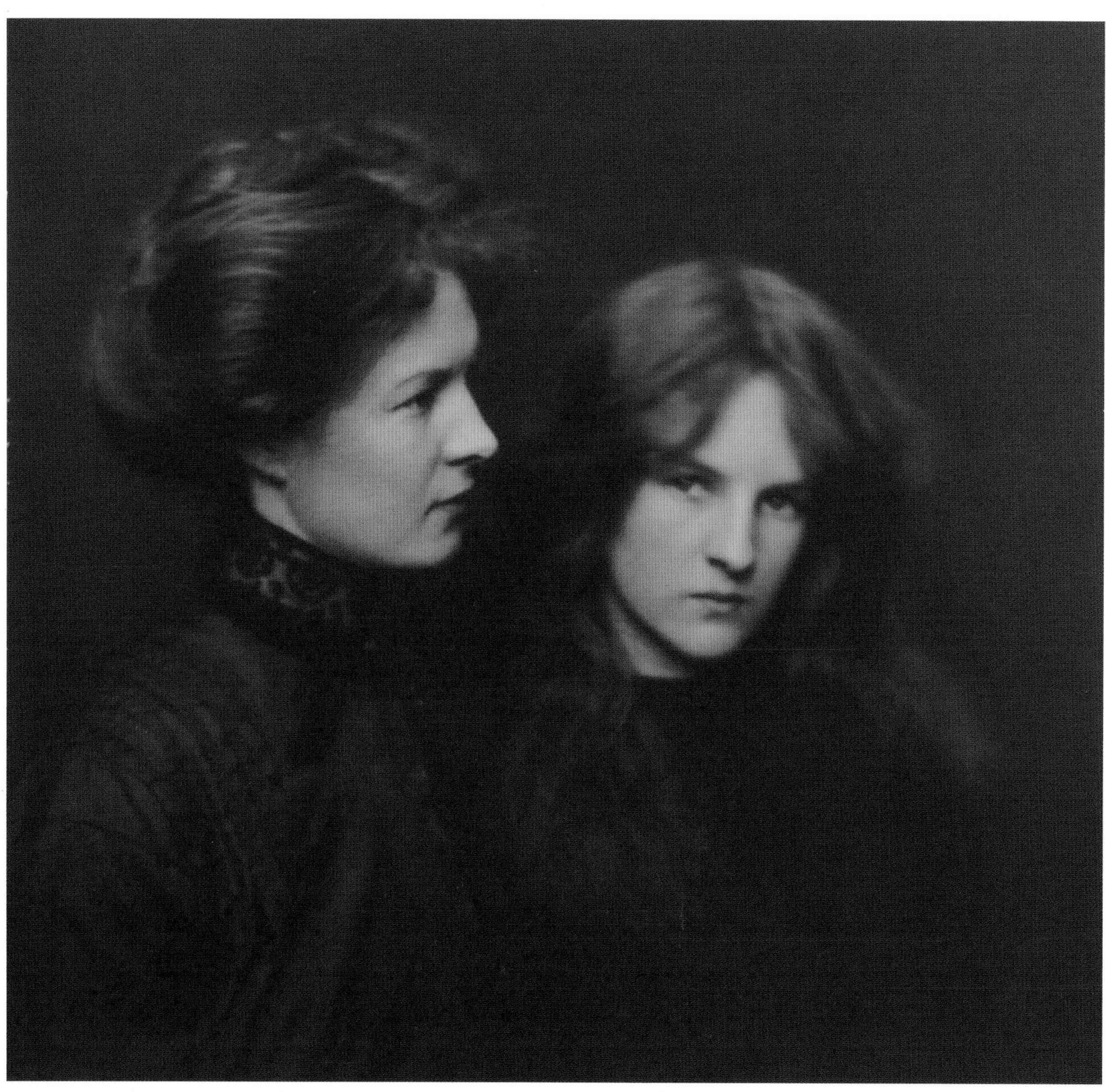

Sisters c.1906
nla.cat-vn282740

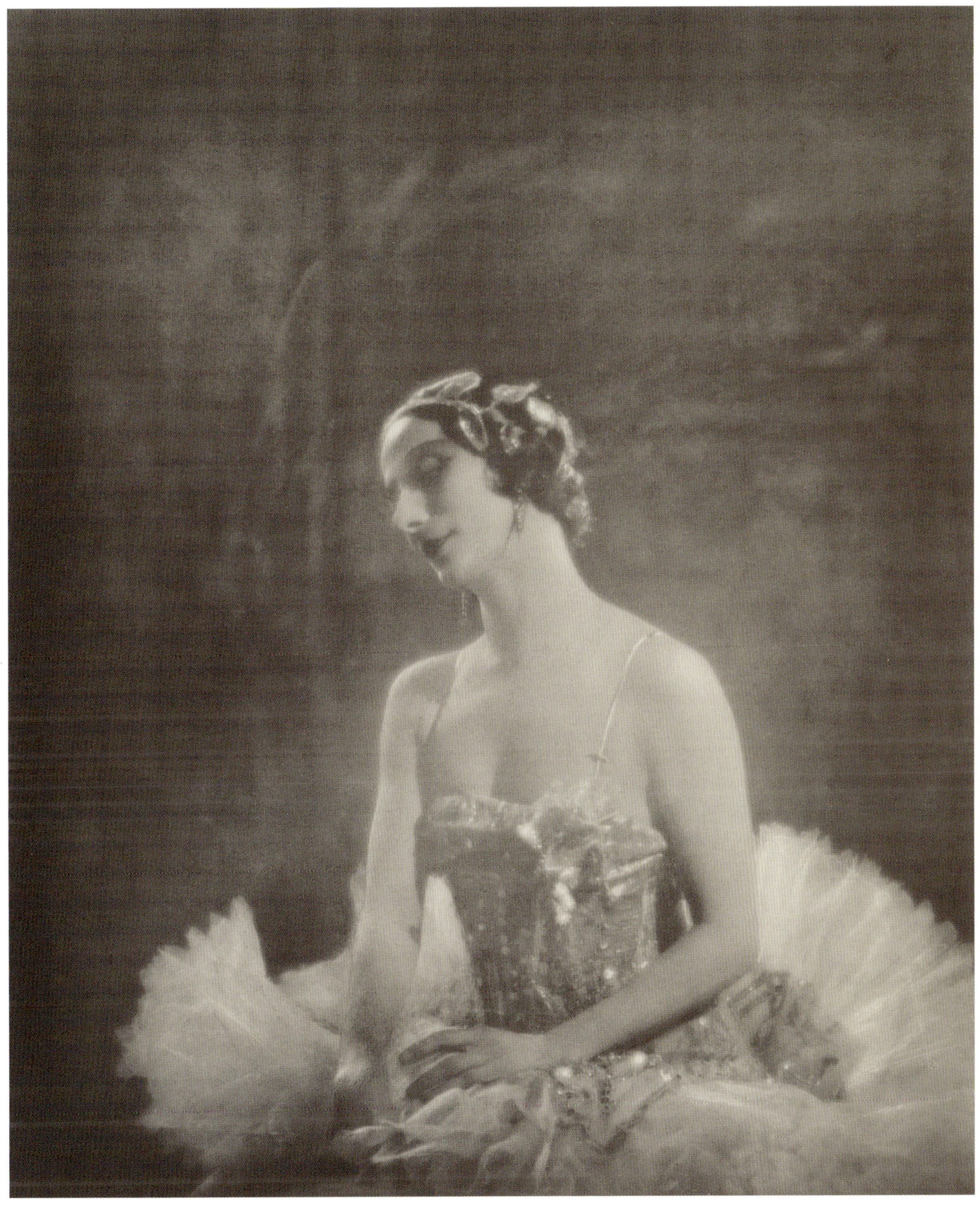

Anna Pavlova 1926
nla.cat-vn1986626

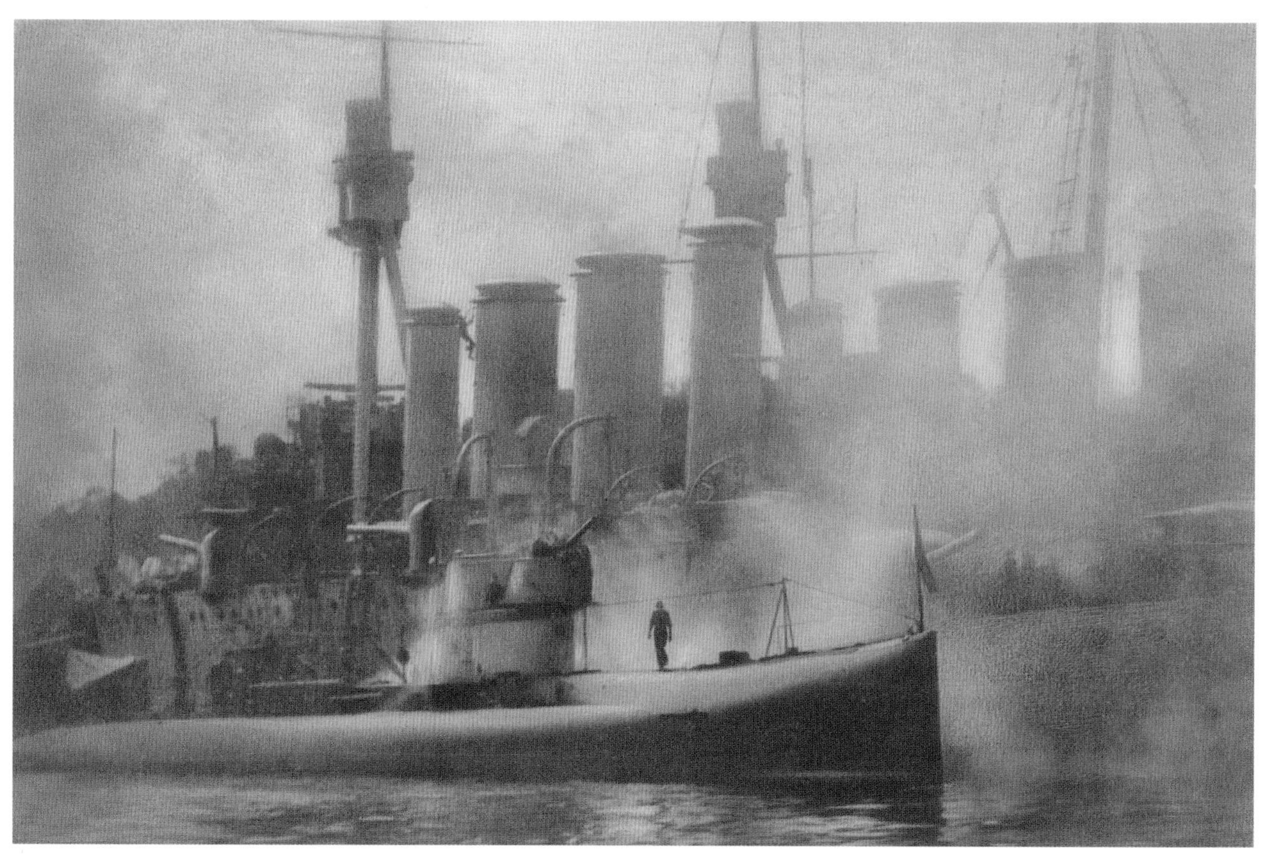

Ye Mariners of England c.1920
nla.cat-vn463929

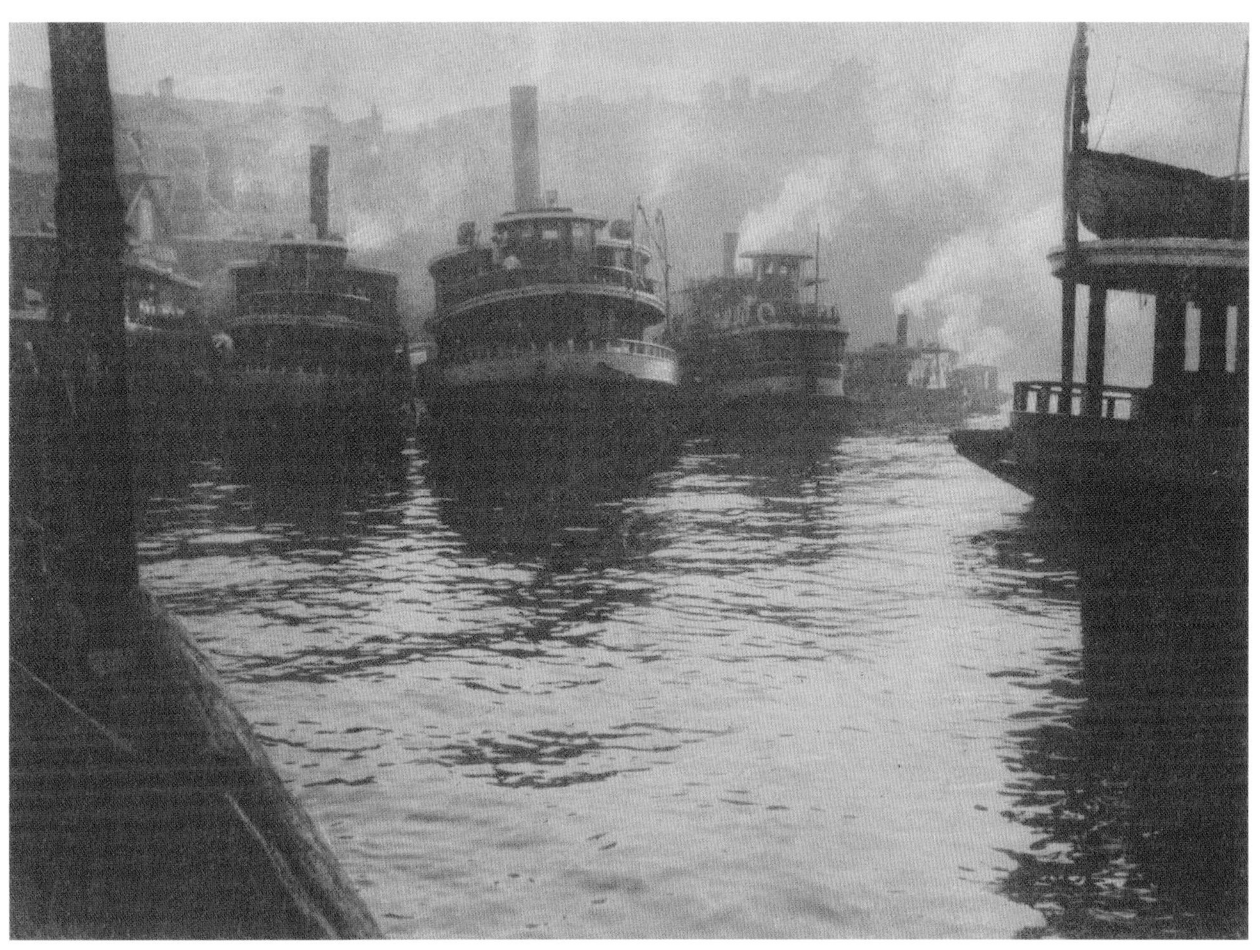

Ferries, Old Milson's Point c.1920s
nla.cat-vn1987108

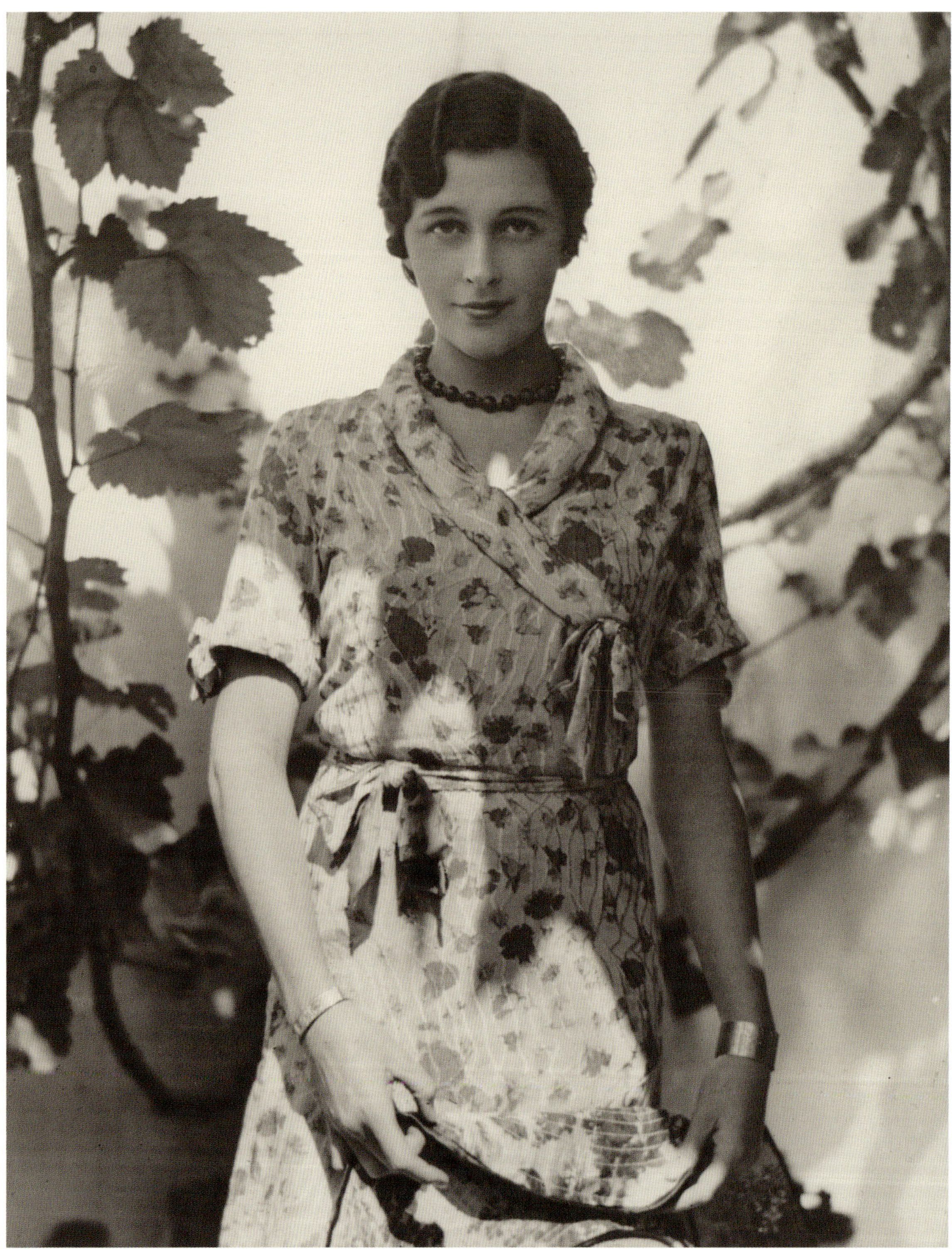

Autumn Leaves 1931
nla.cat-vn464019

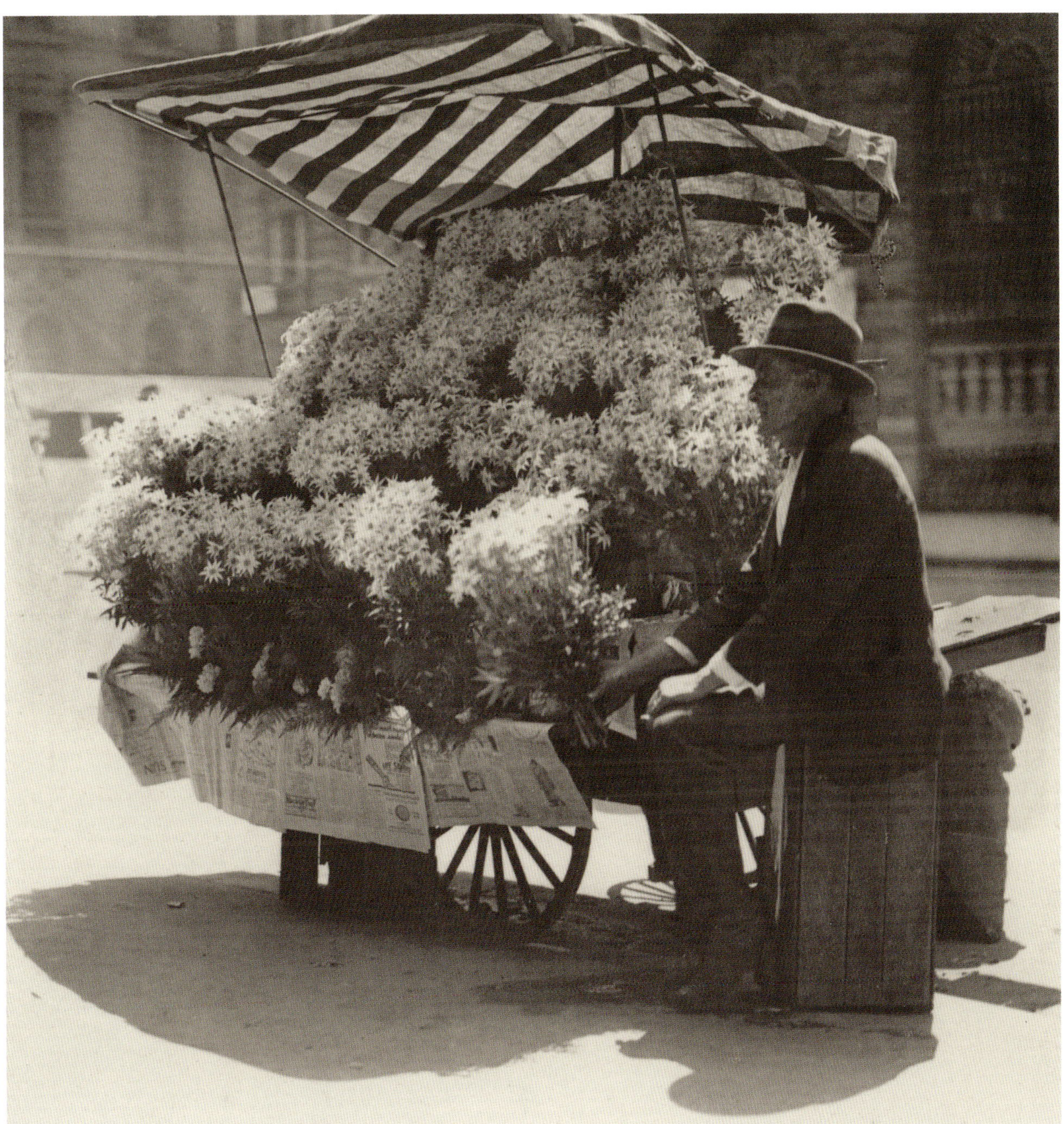

Flower Seller, Martin Place, Sydney c.1910
nla.cat-vn464539

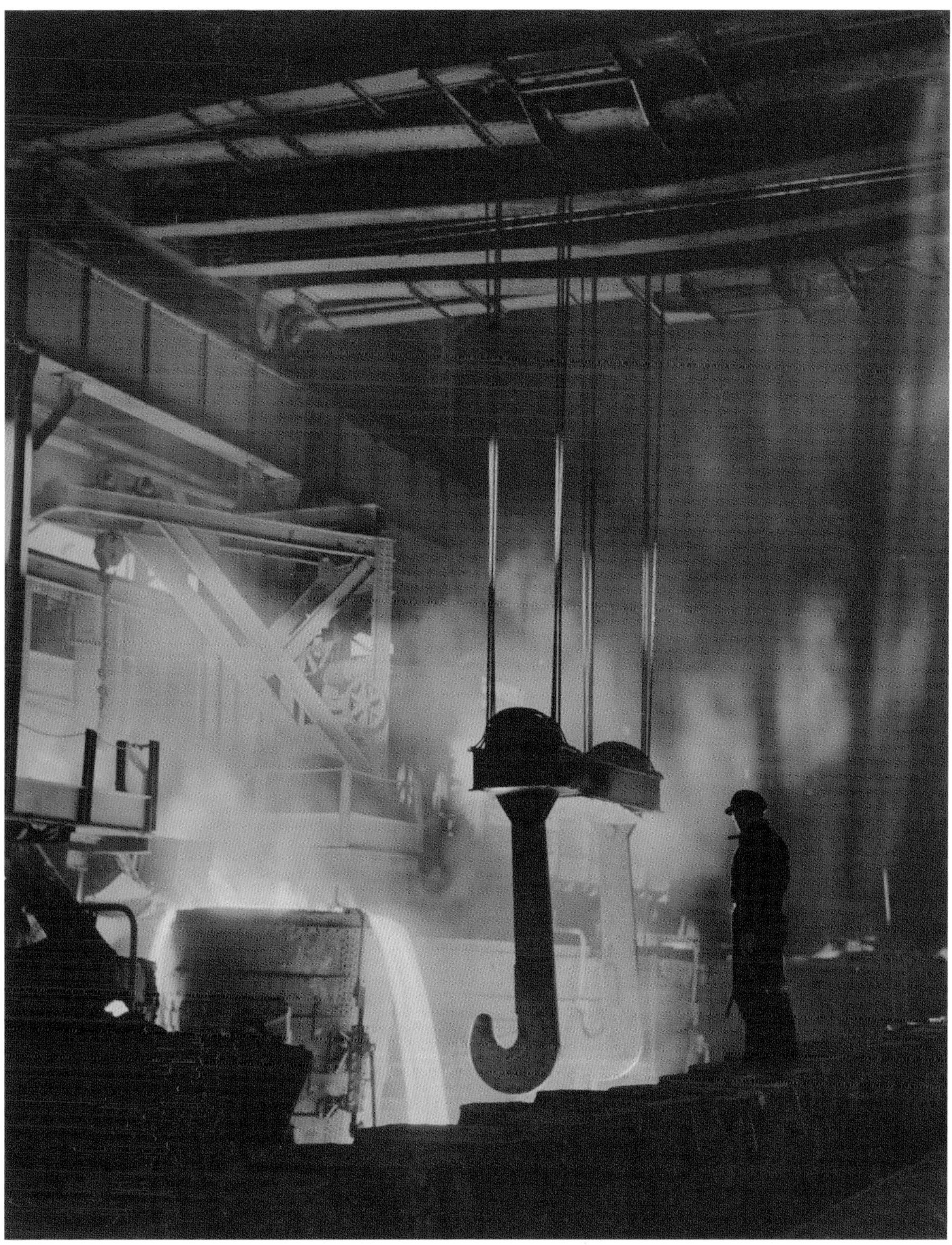

Pouring Steel, NSW 1934
nla.cat-vn1984080

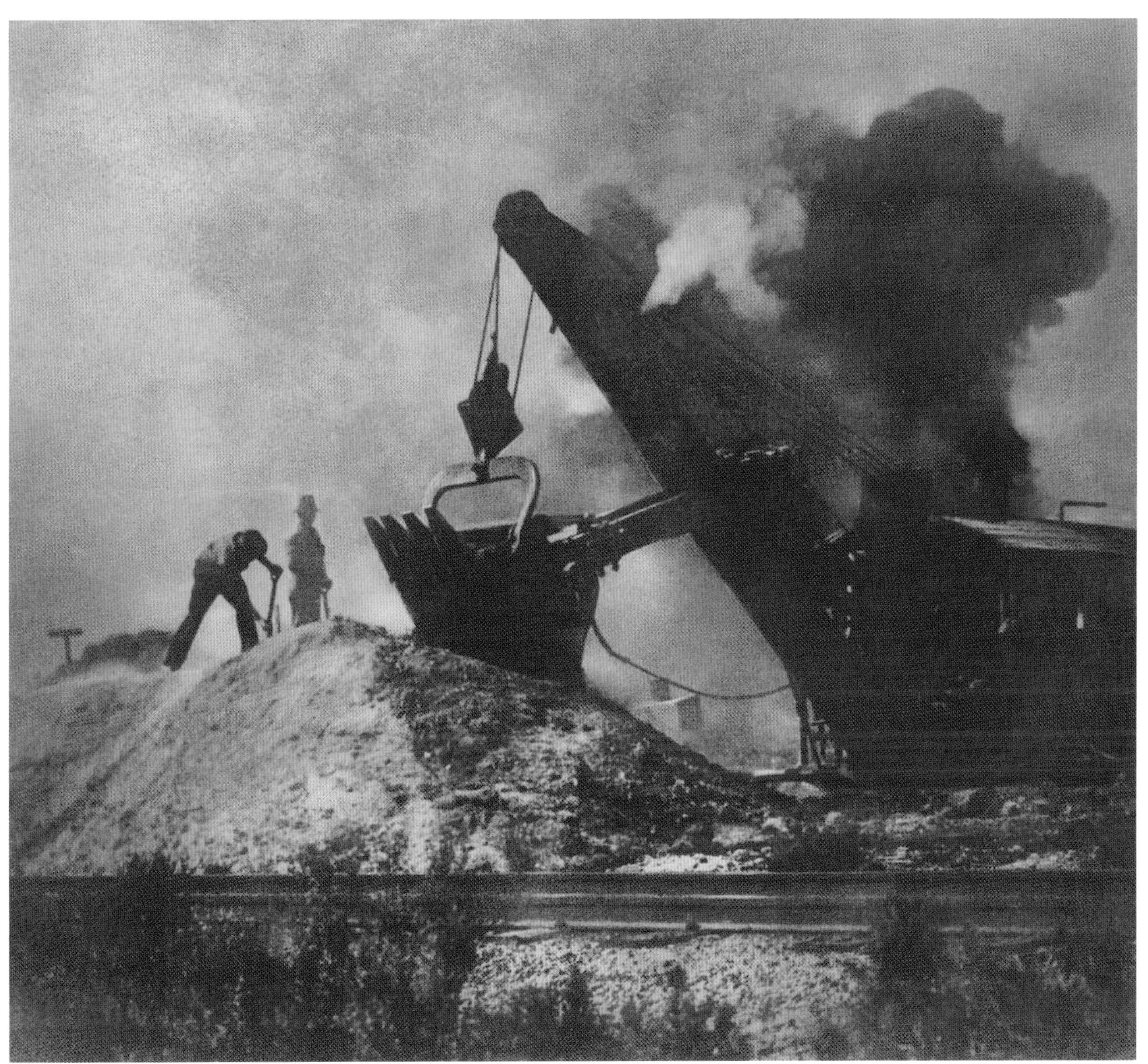

Laying the Track 1935
nla.cat-vn461606

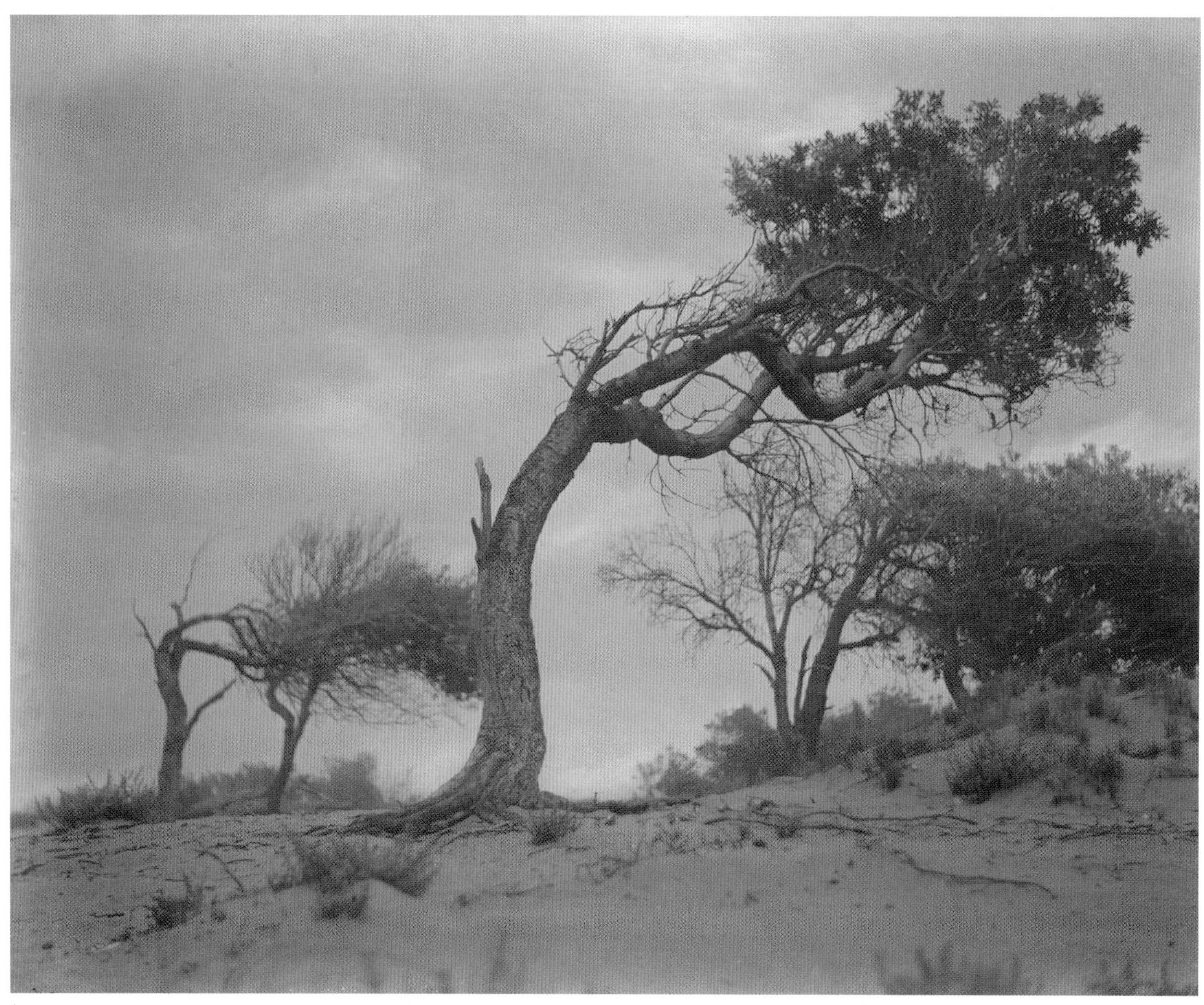

The Bent Trees 1915
nla.cat-vn3044977

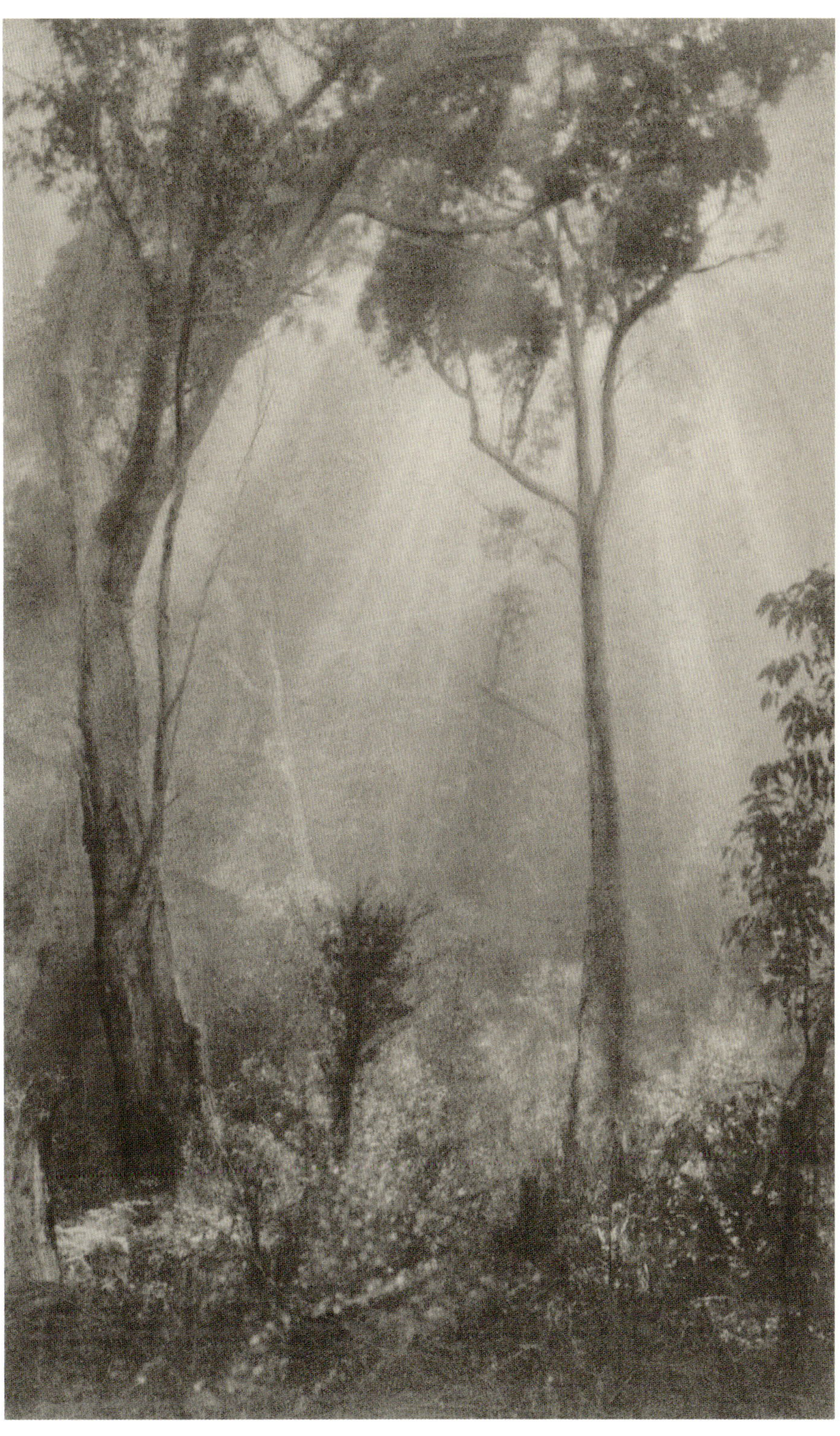

The Veil, Blue Mountains, New South Wales 1915
nla.cat-vn464780

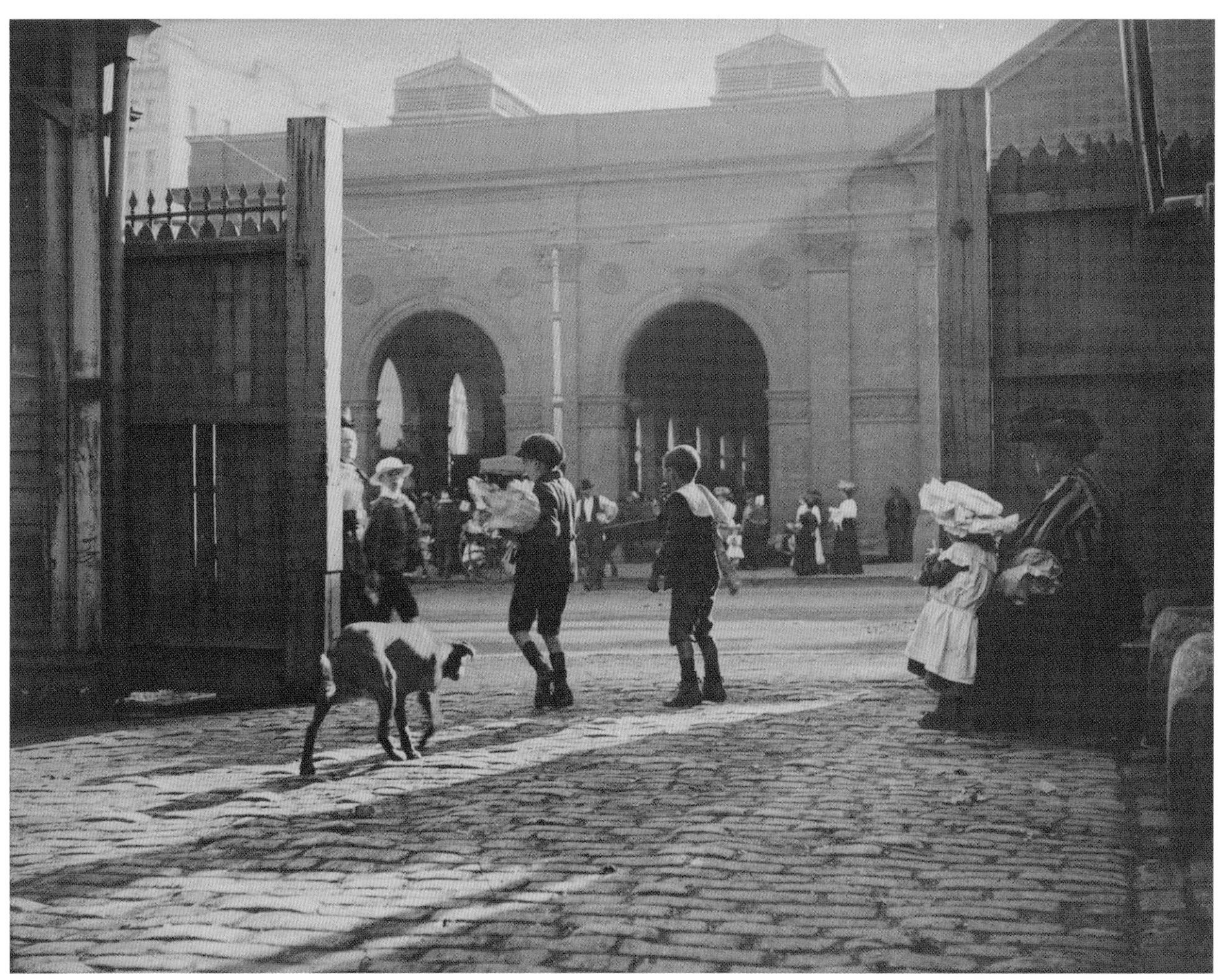

Old Belmore Markets, Sydney c.1905
nla.cat-vn1987175

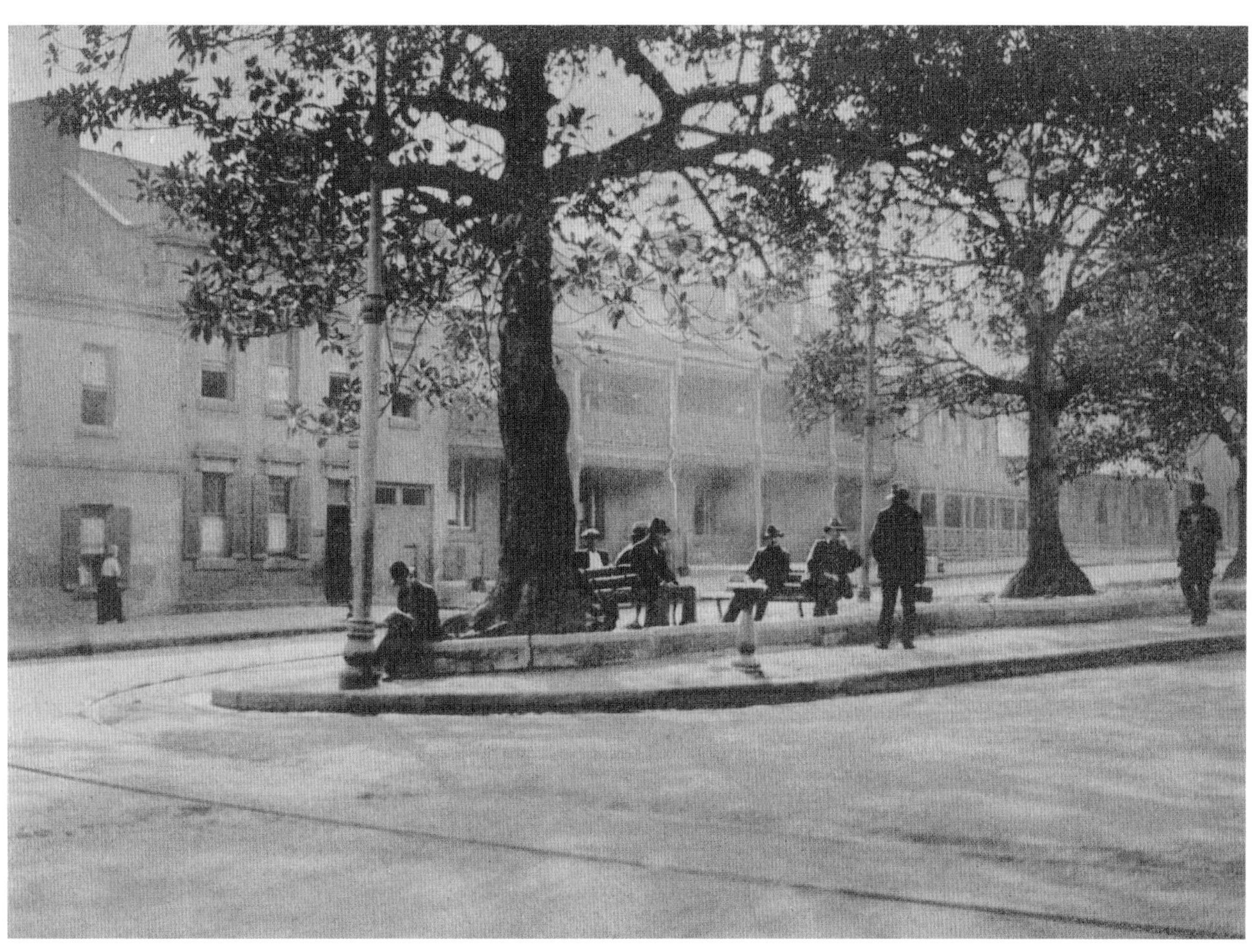

Tram Terminus in Lower Fort St., Millers Point, Sydney c.1910
nla.cat-vn1987166

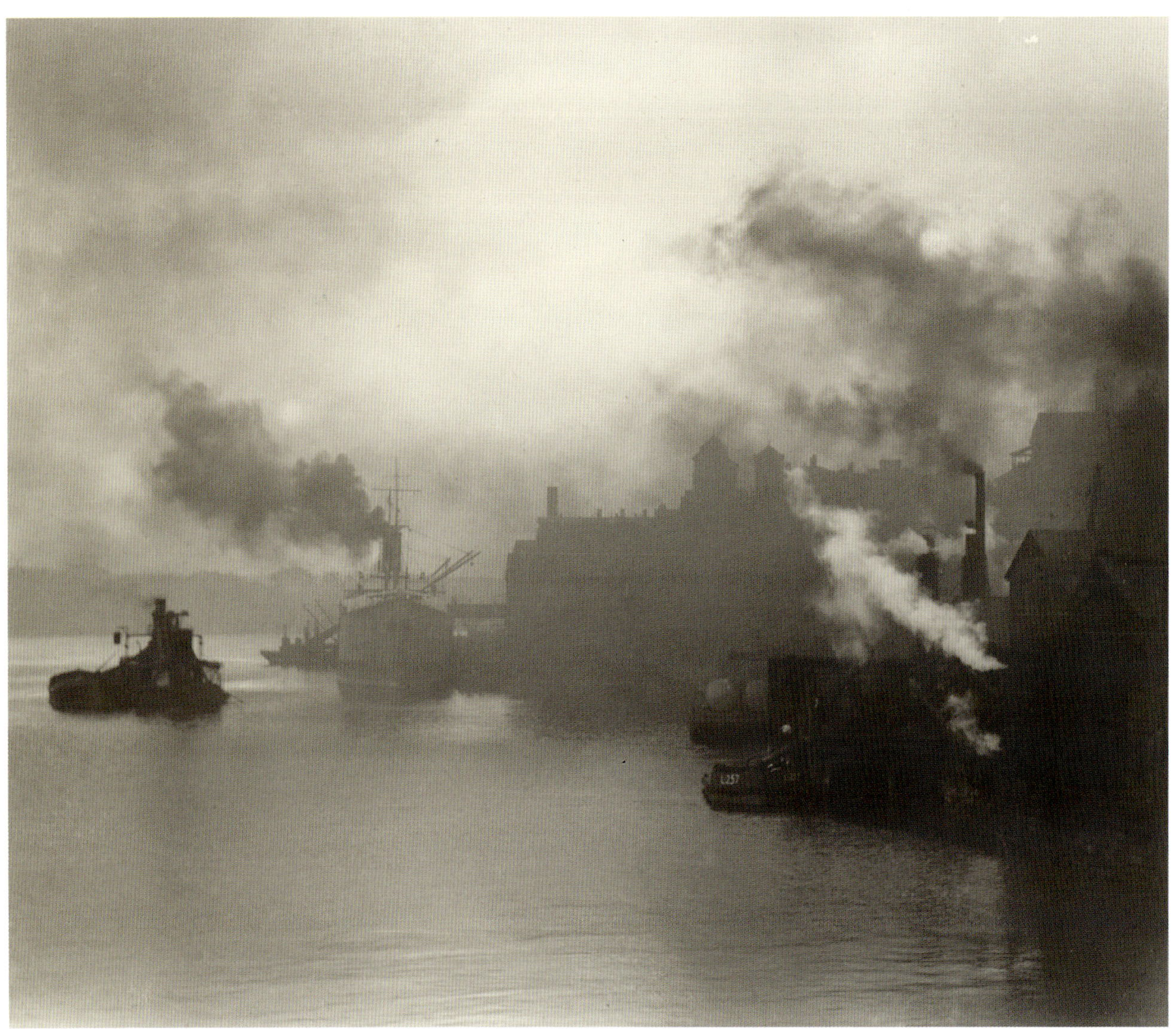

A Sydney Waterside c.1925
nla.cat-vn463939

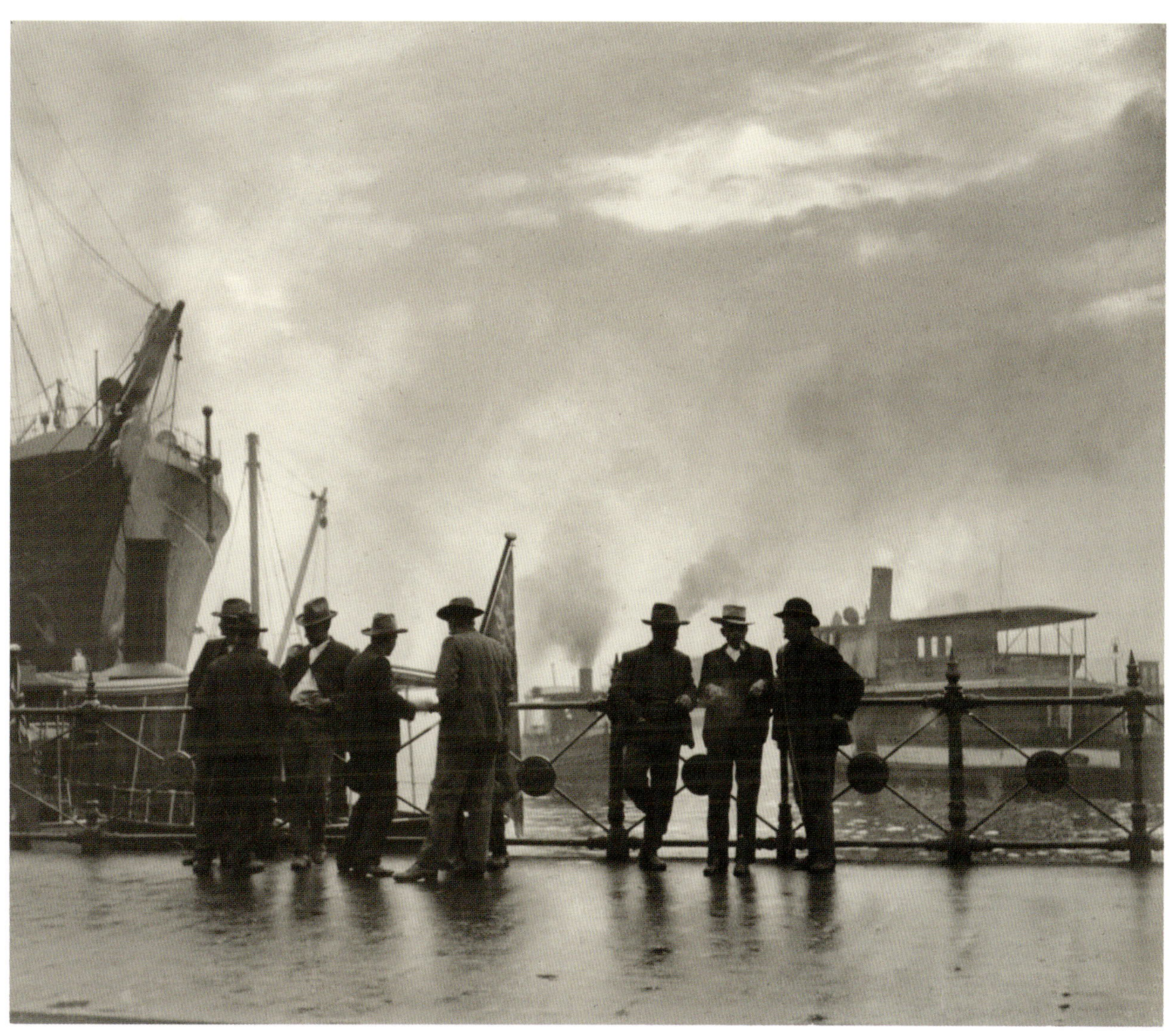

Wharfies, Circular Quay 1910
nla.cat-vn464572

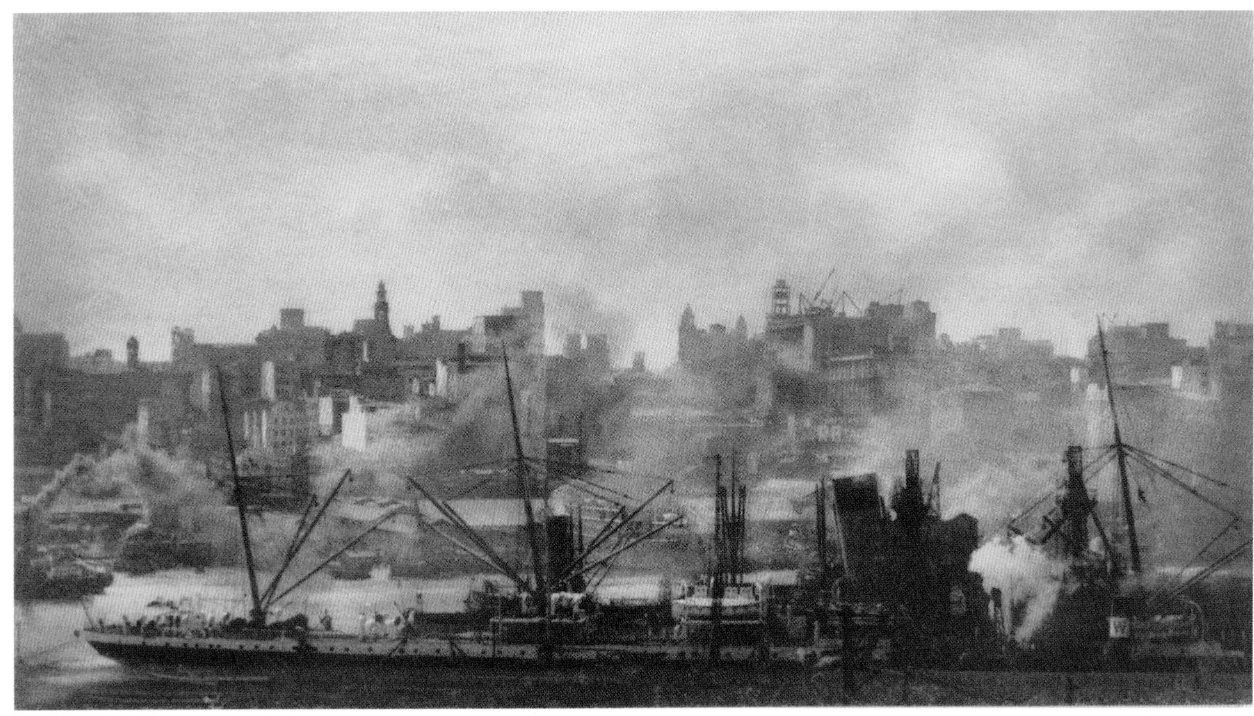

Sydney Skyline, from Darling Harbour, NSW c.1929
nla.cat-vn441280

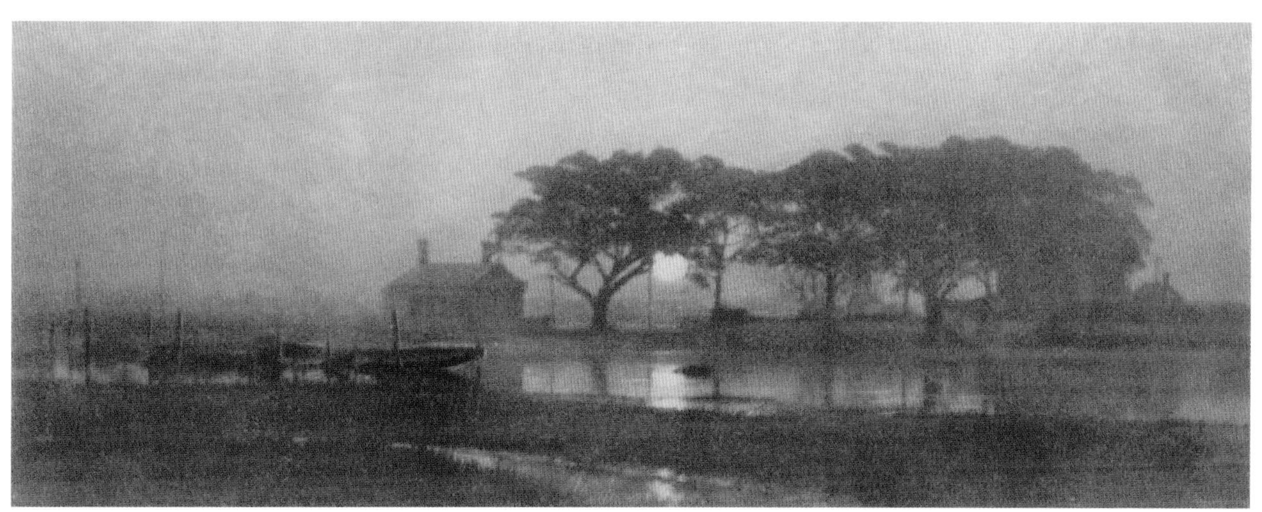

Moonrise c.1935
nla.cat-vn1987367

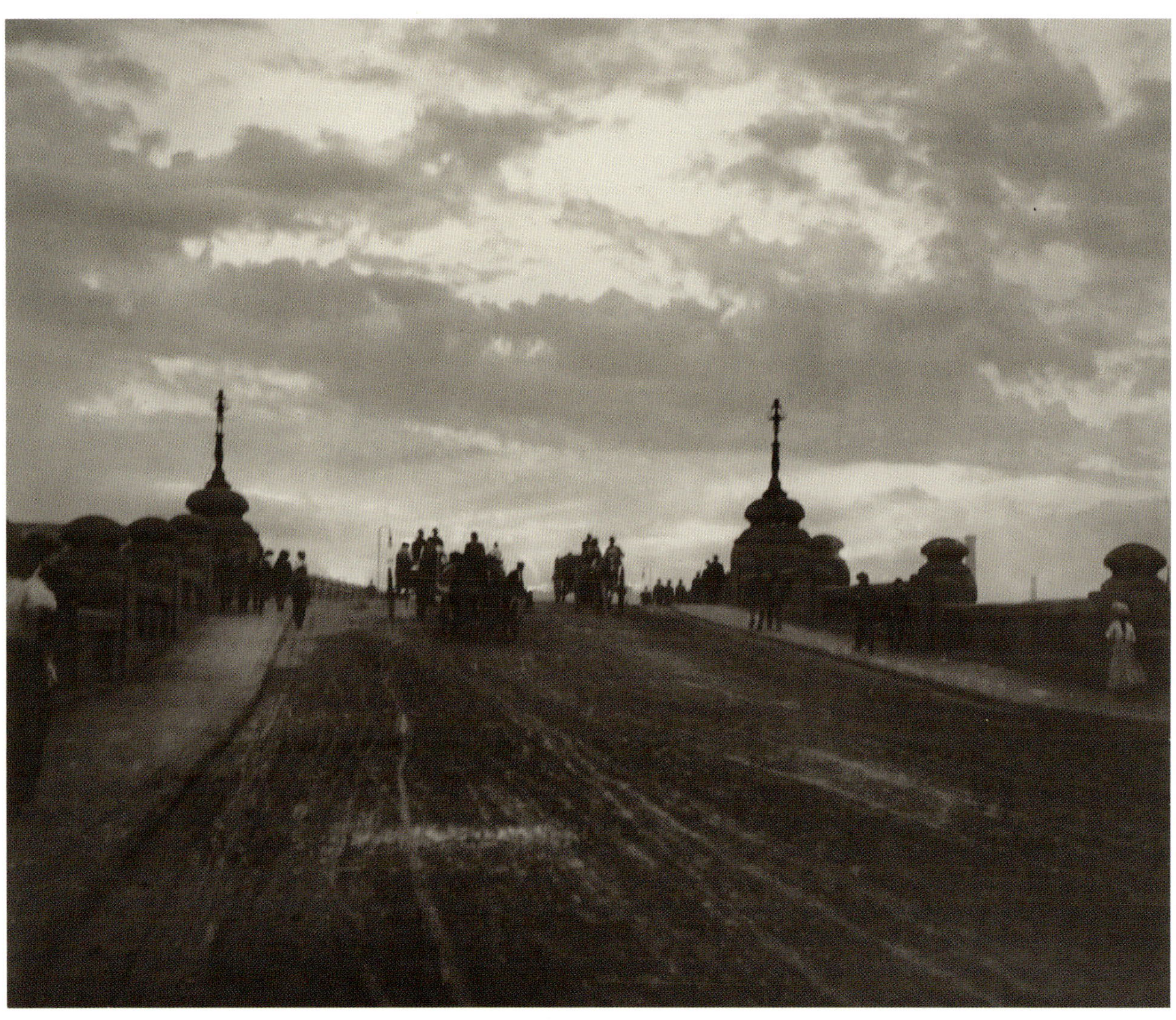

Winter Evening, Pyrmont Bridge 1911
nla.cat-vn451612

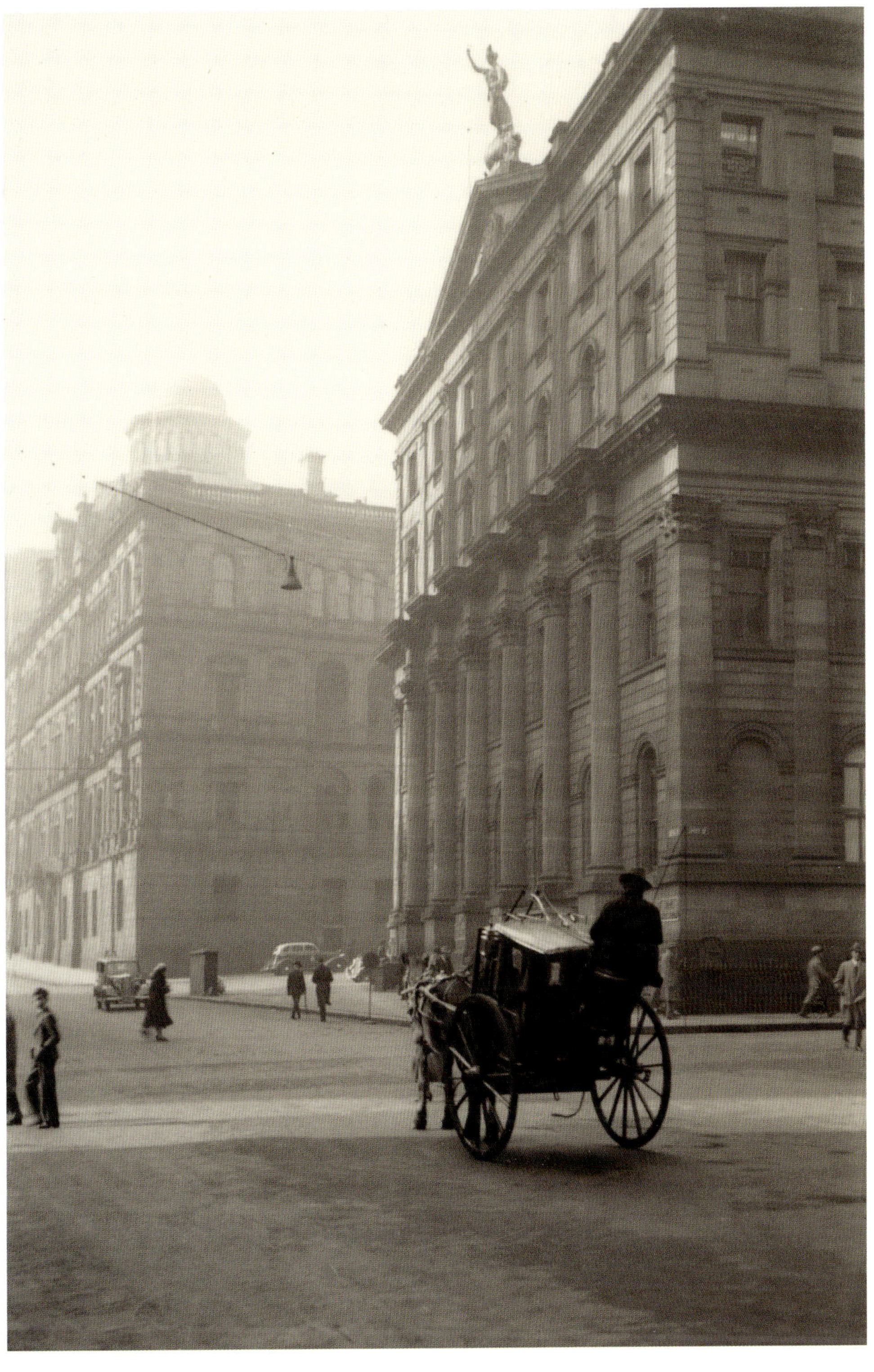

The Royal Exchange c.1935
nla.cat-vn3044977

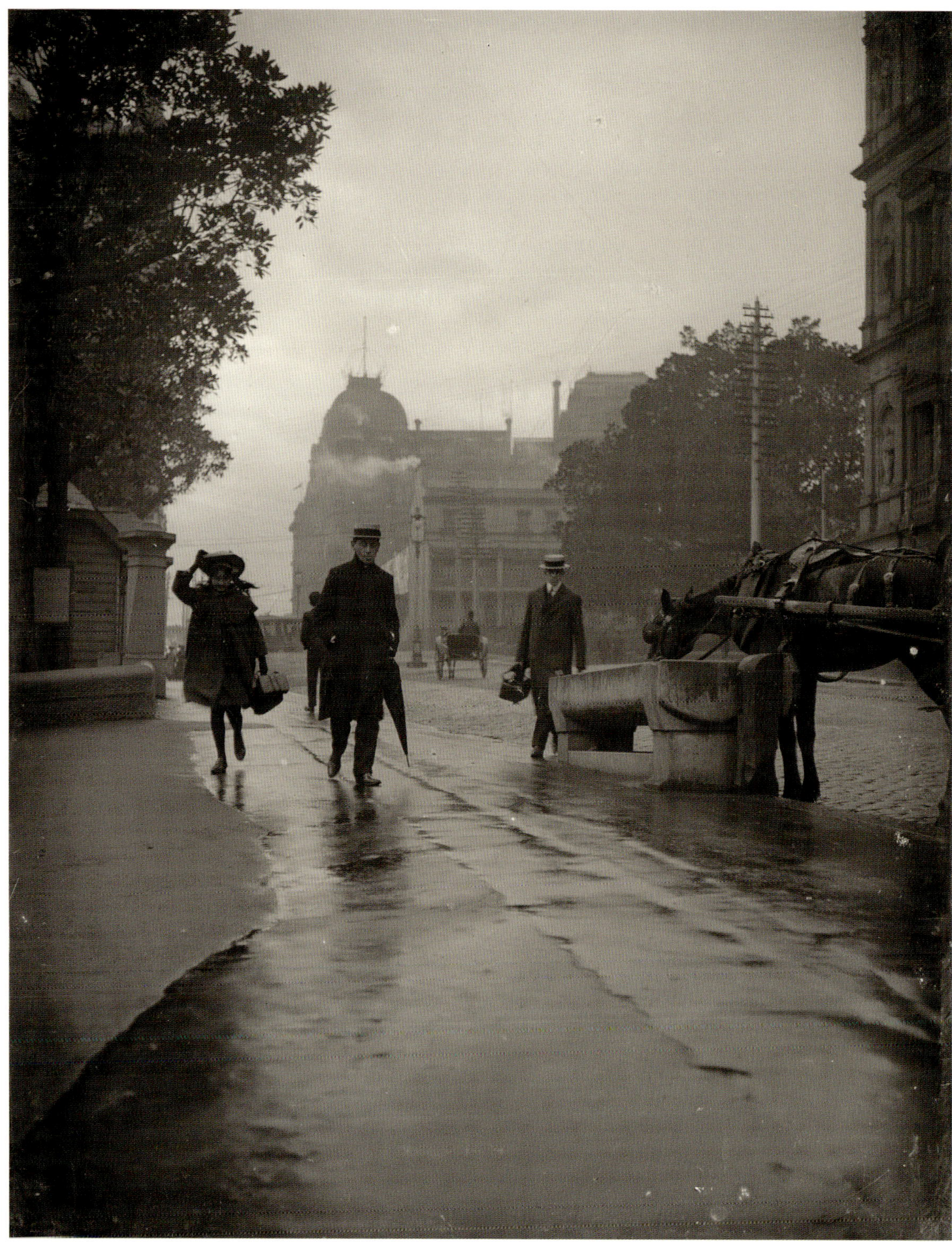

Wet Day, Bridge Street, Sydney between 1910 and 1940
nla.cat-vn3775480

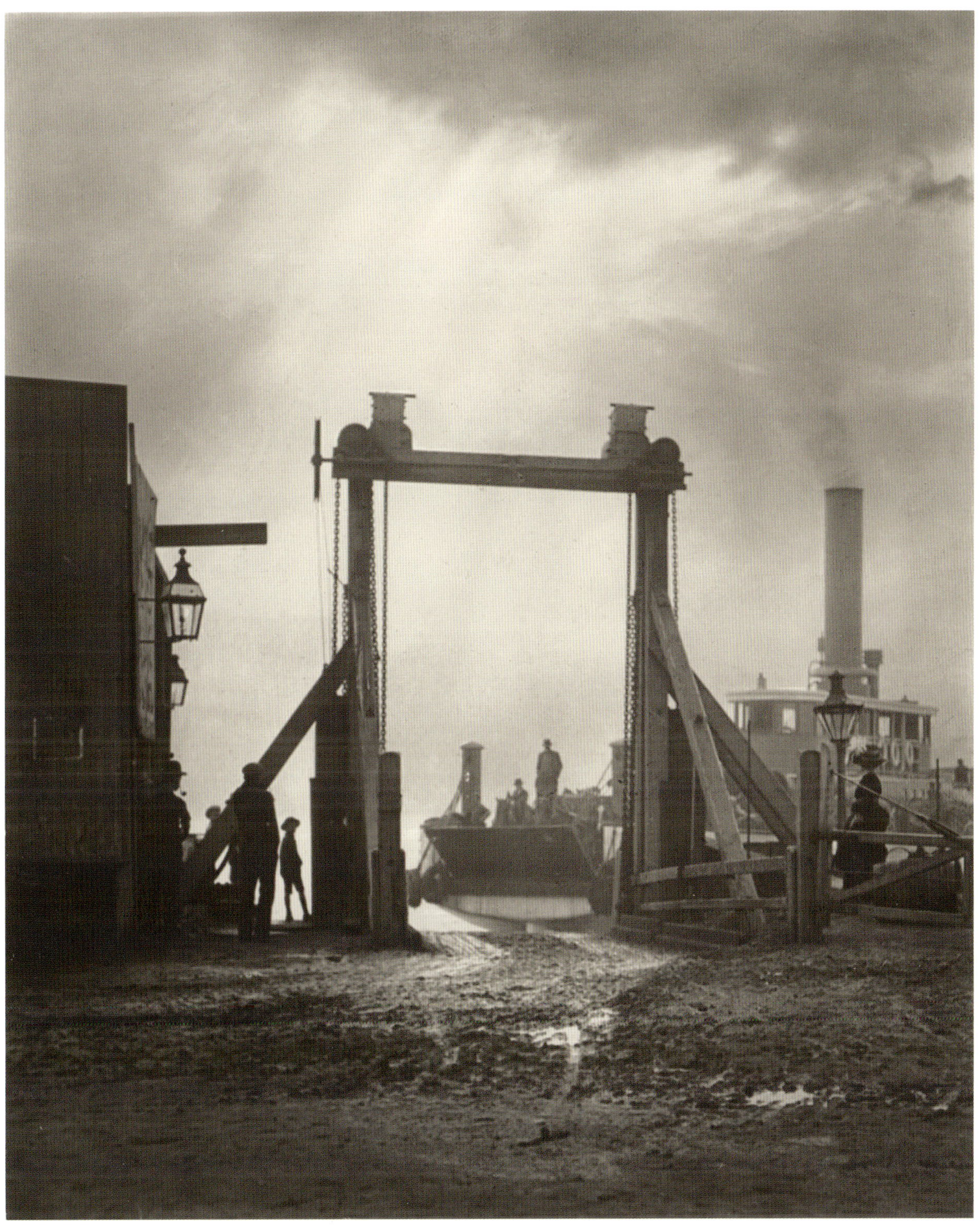

Horse Ferry, Milson's Point 1908
nla.cat-vn1987081

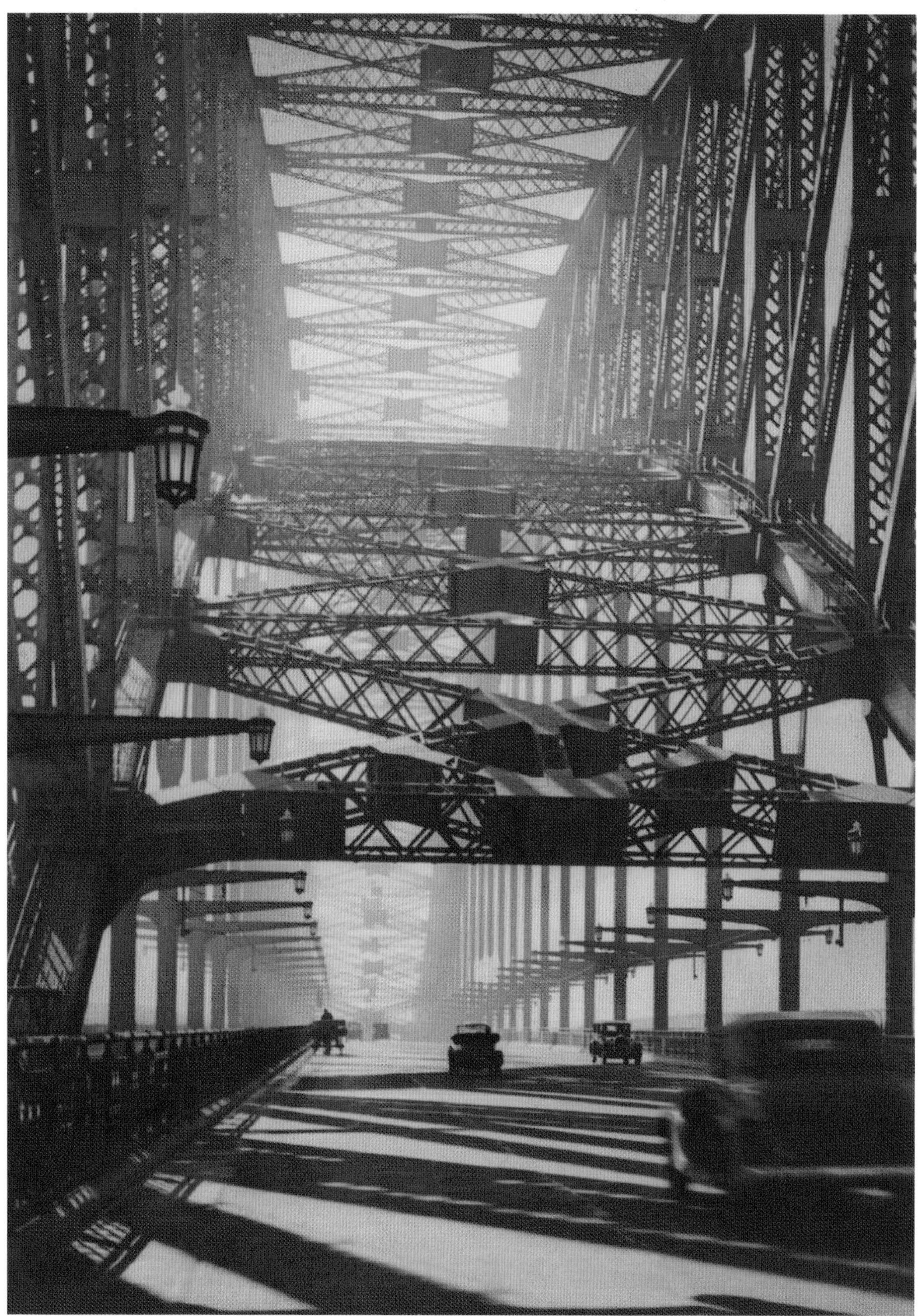

Arch of Steel 1933
nla.cat-vn1983974

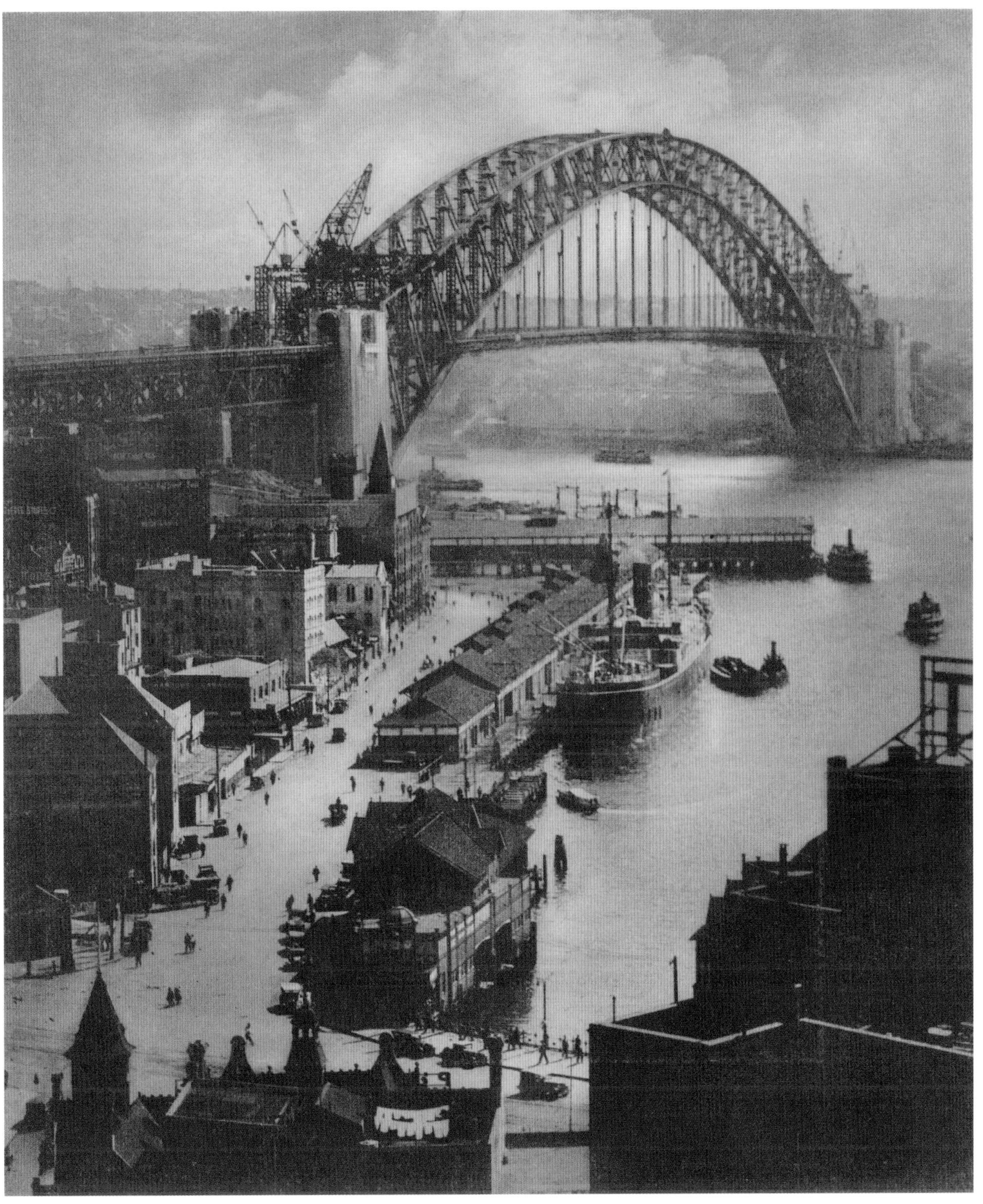

Circular Quay West 1931
nla.cat-vn461467

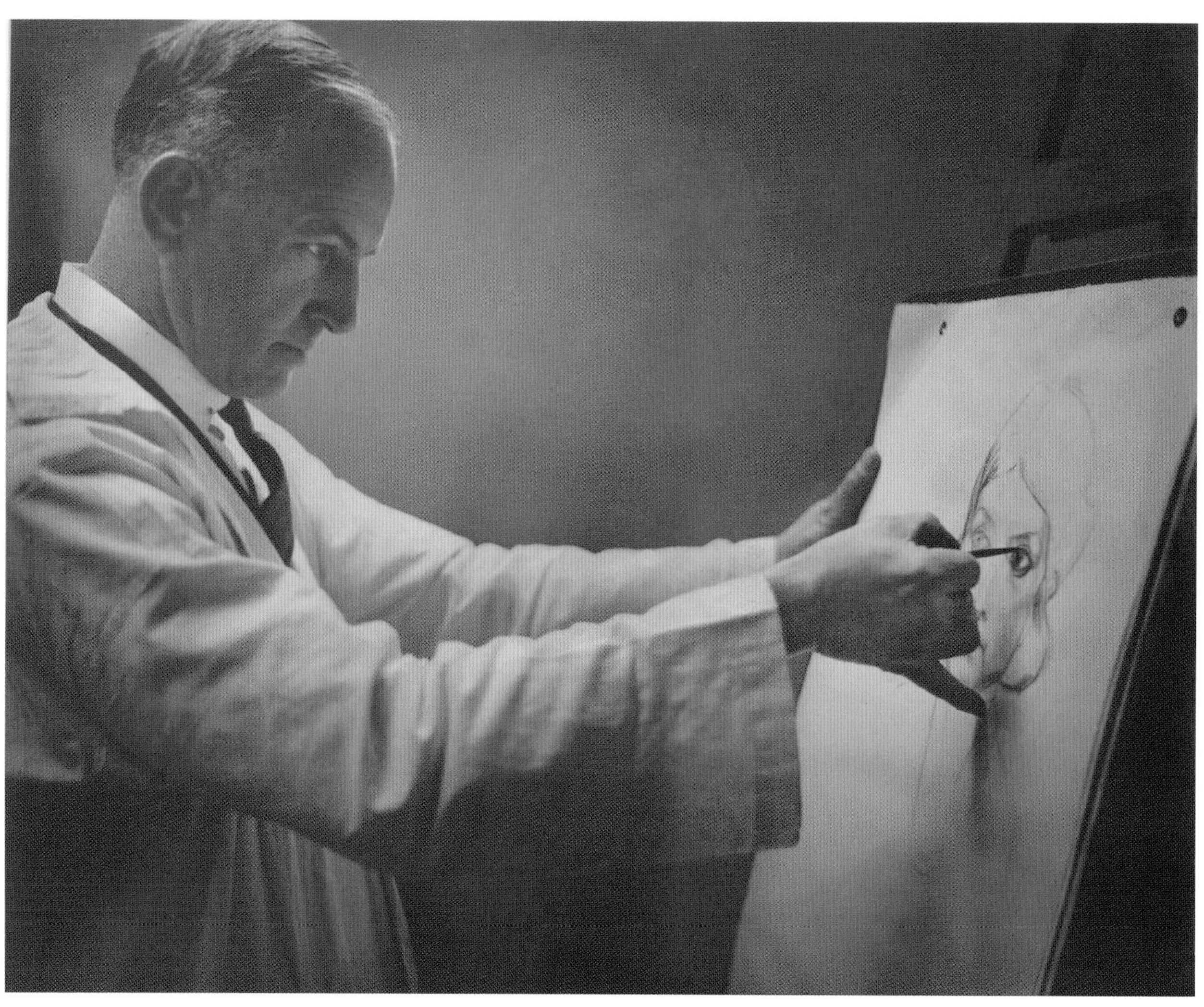

Charcoal Drawing 1931
nla.cat-vn464229

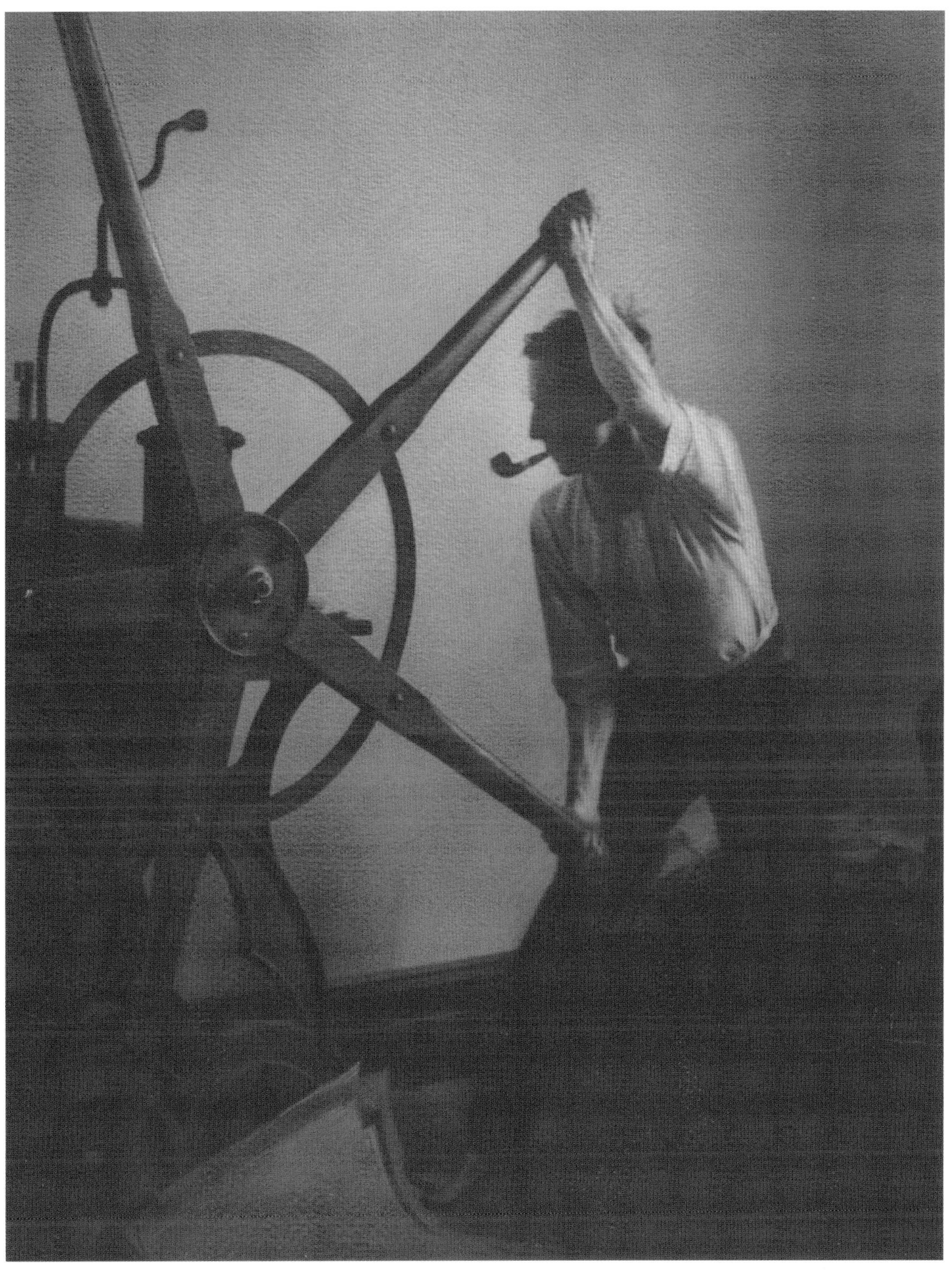

Pulling the Proof between 1914 and 1915
nla.cat-vn1986757

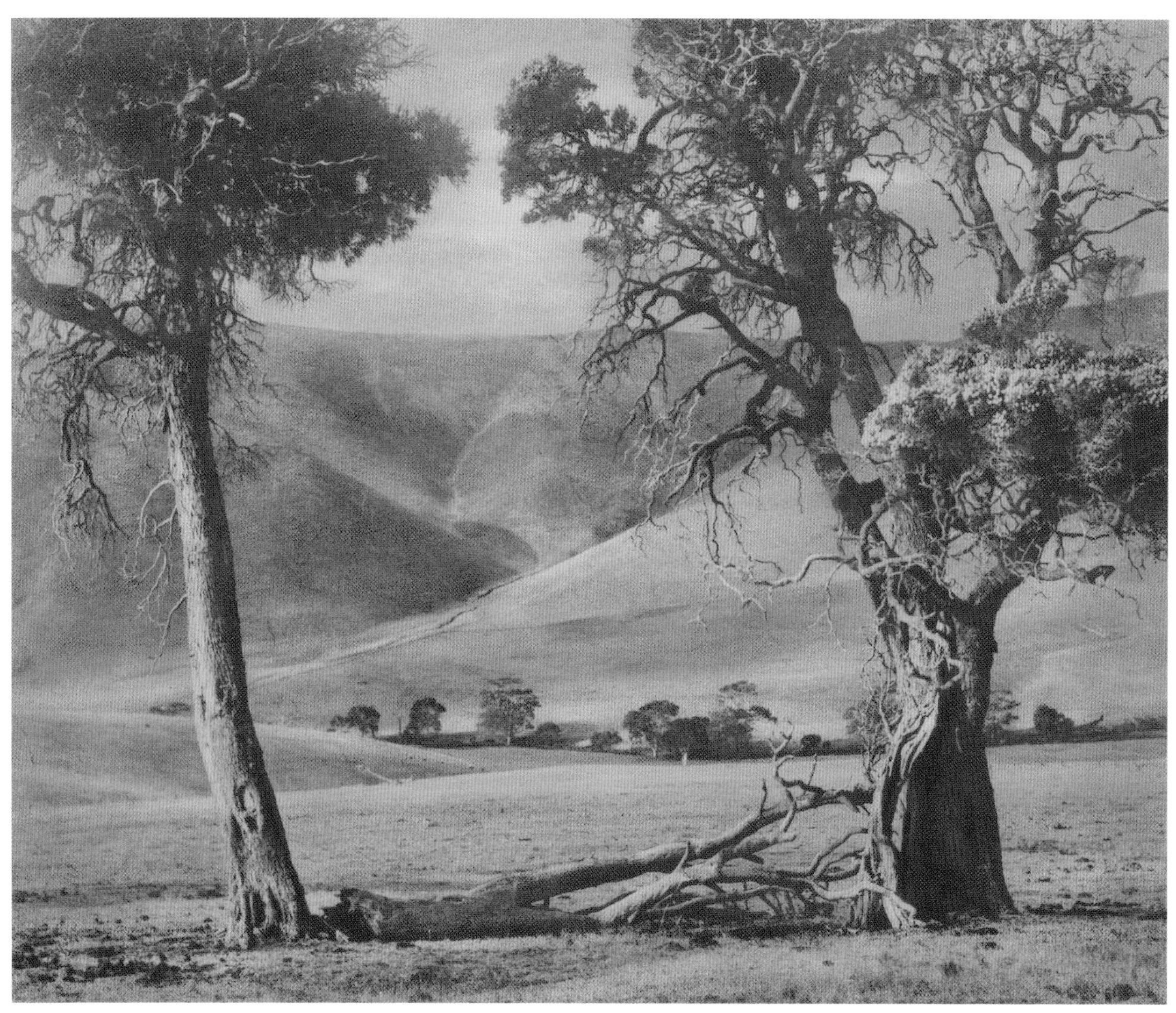

A Valley, Rapid Bay, South Australia 1937
nla.cat-vn464865

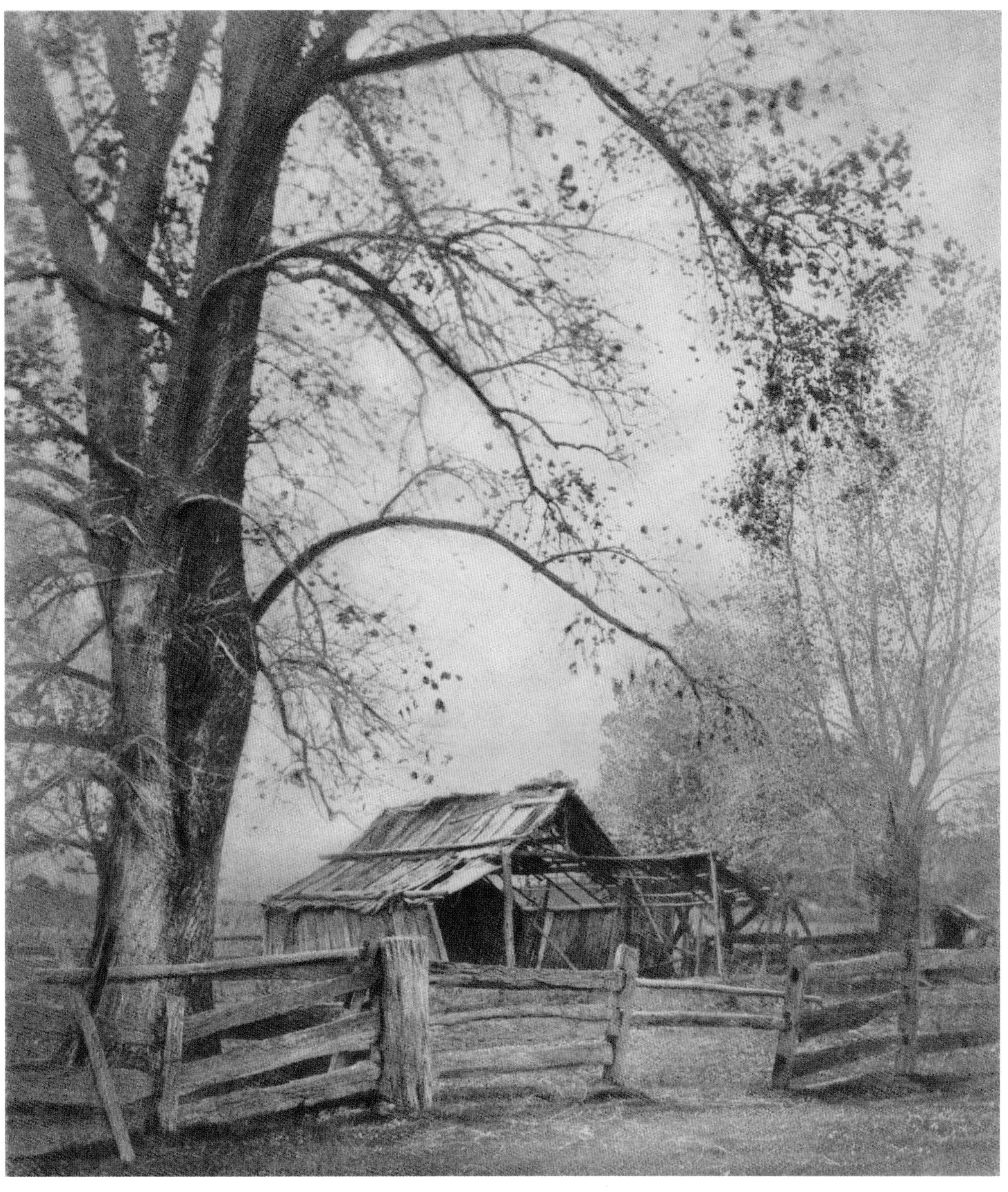

Autumn 1934
nla.cat-vn464739

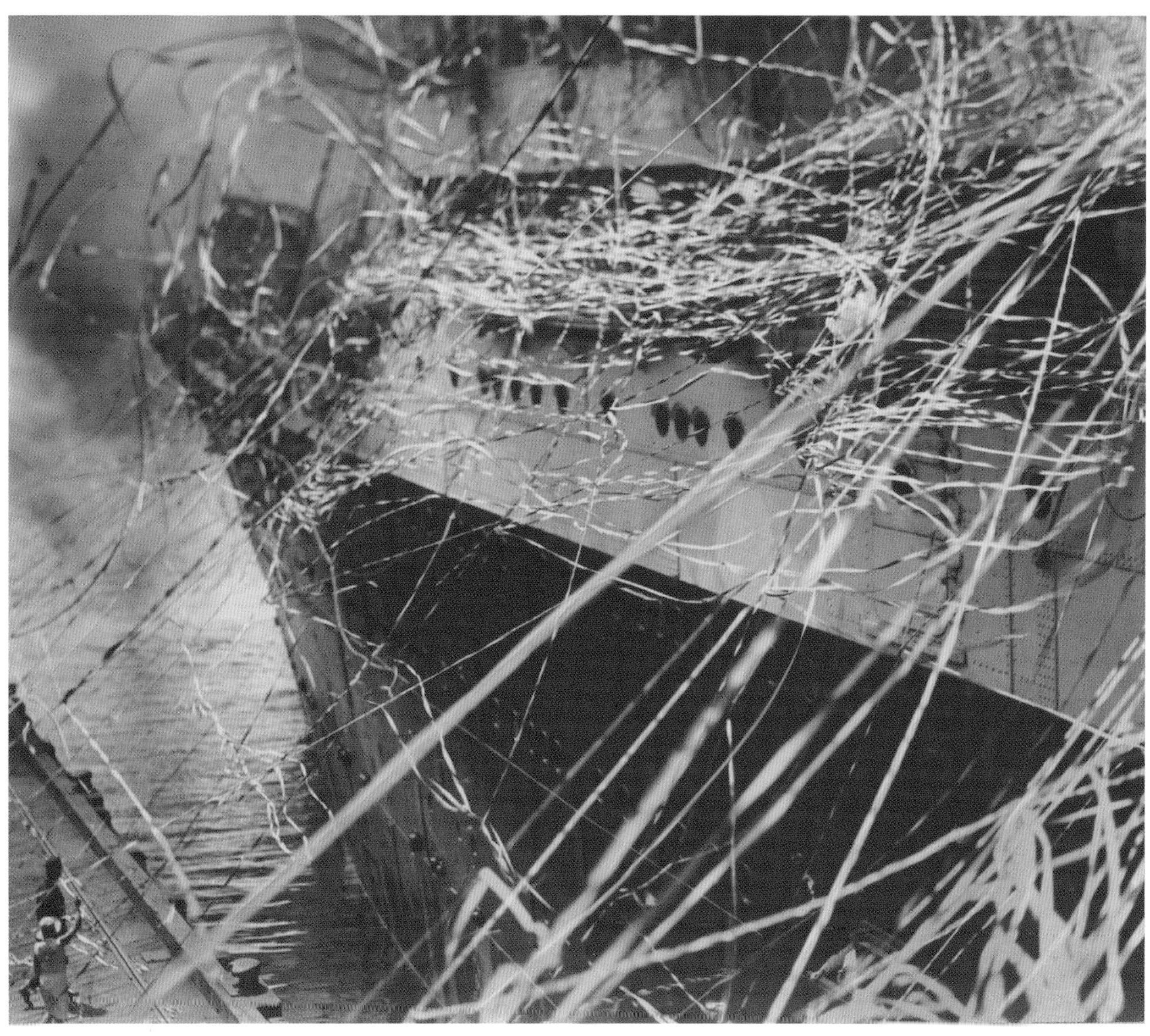

Departure 1928
nla.cat-vn463885

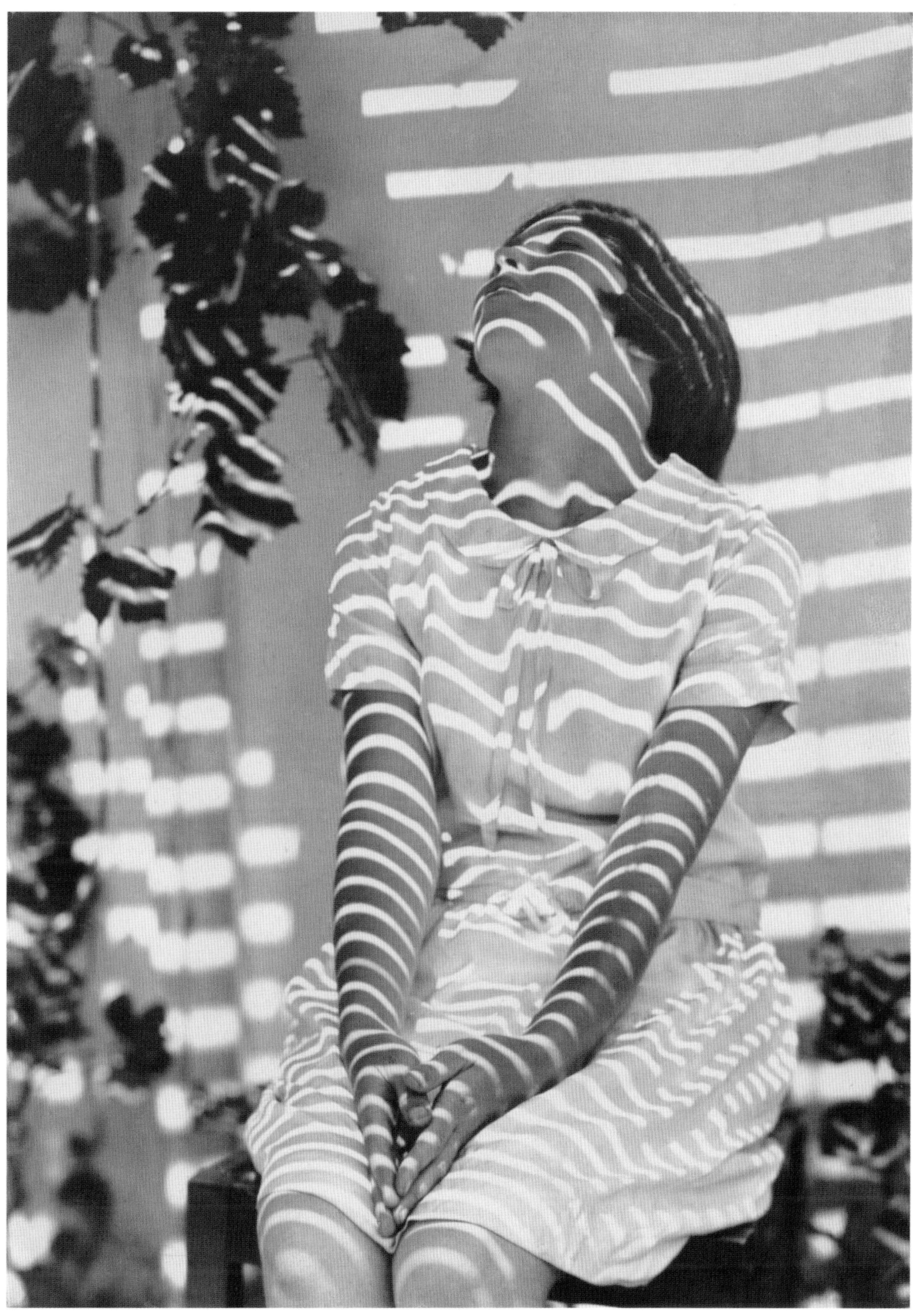

Pergola Pattern 1931
nla.cat-vn464080

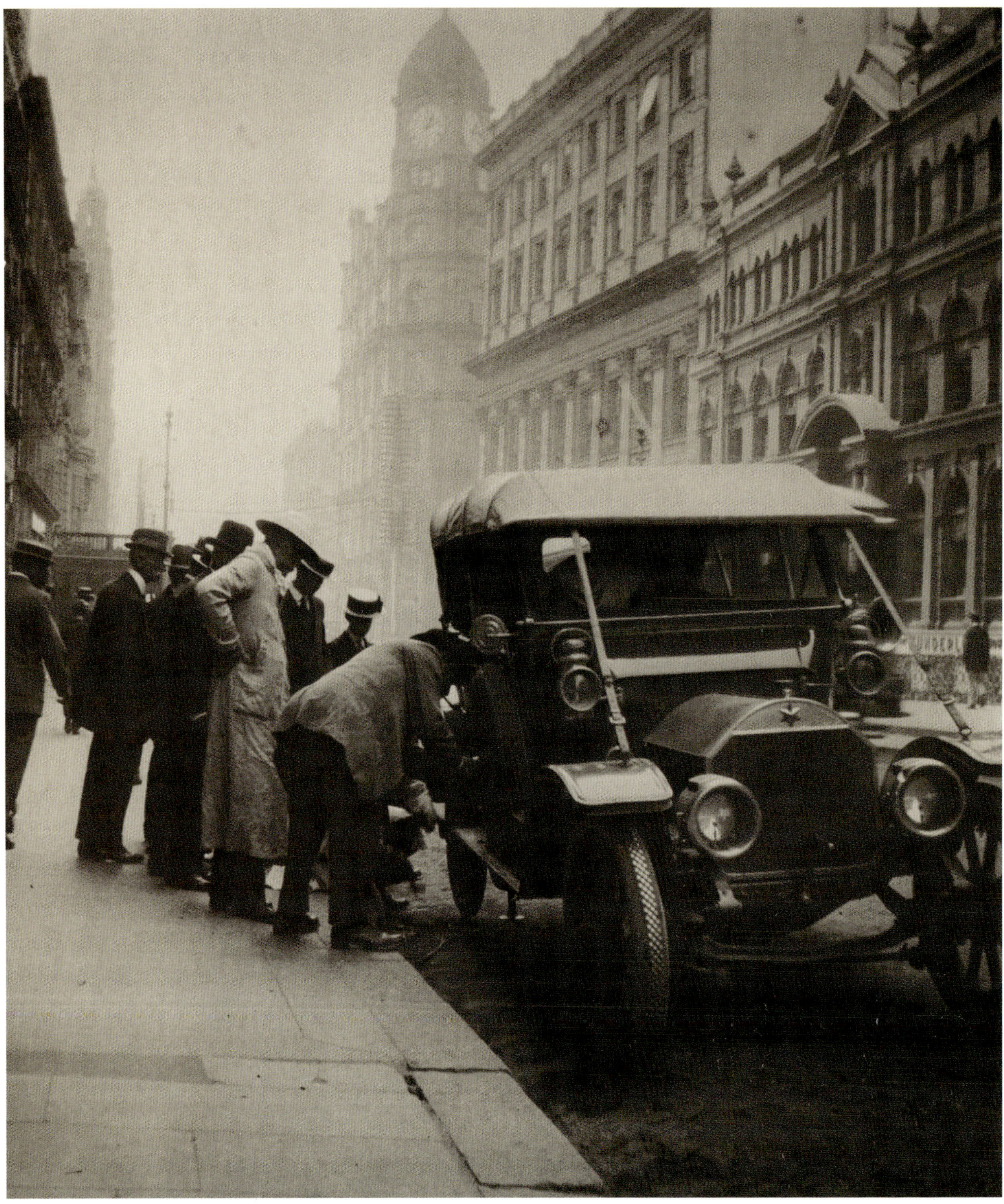

Puncture in Pitt Street c.1912
nla.cat-vn3044977

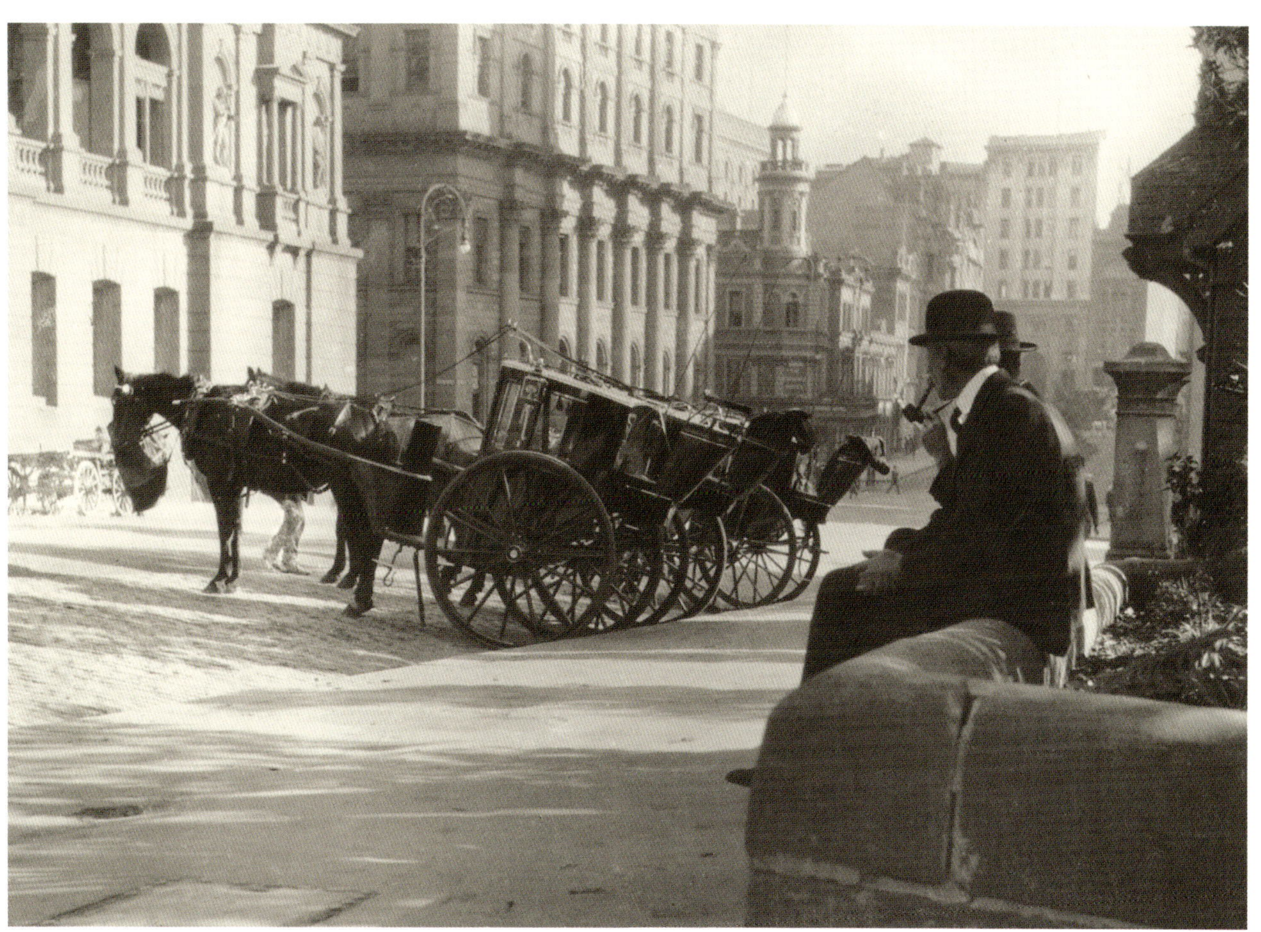

Cabbies, Bridge Street, Sydney, NSW 1904
nla.cat-vn1965502

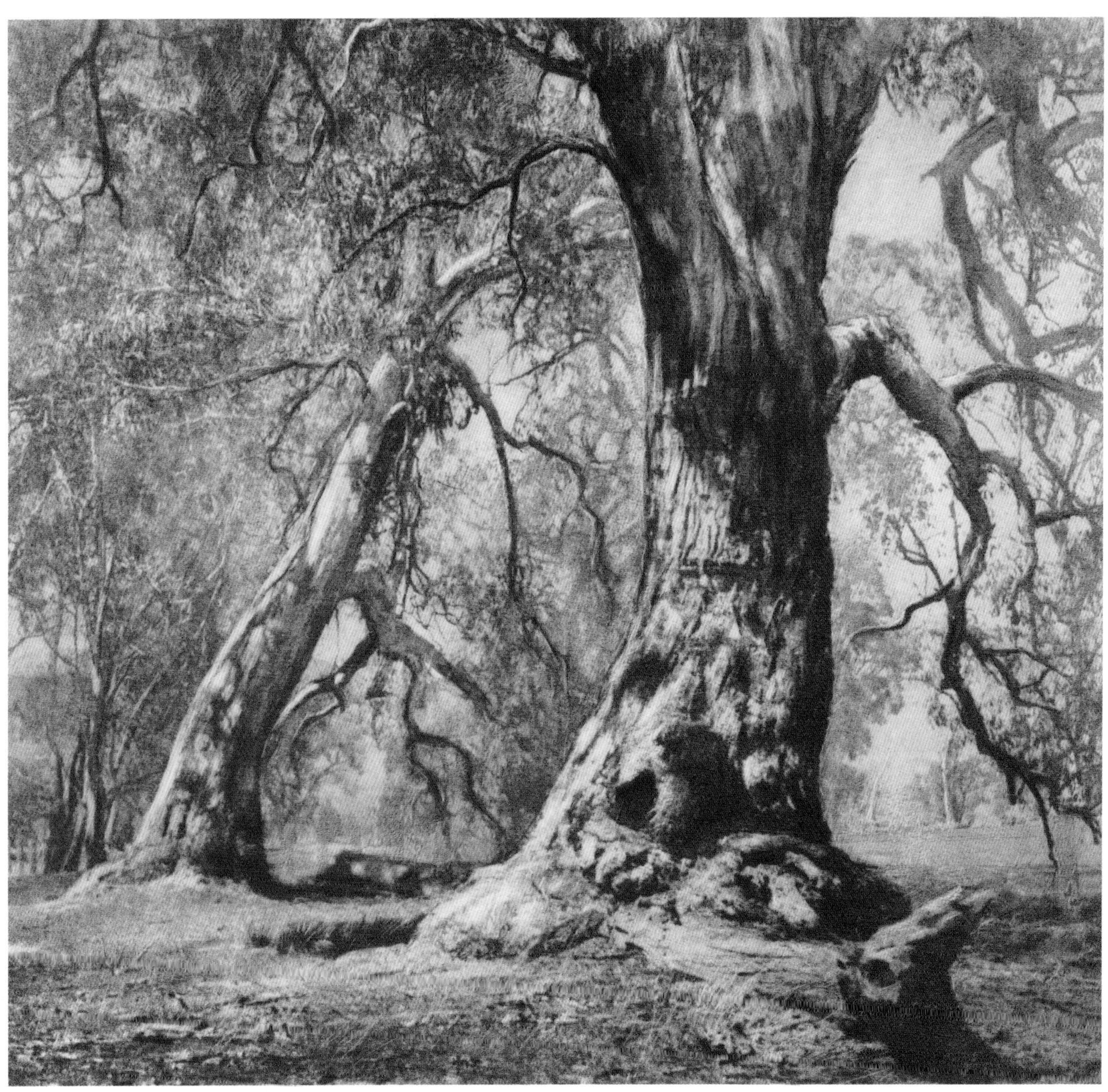

Veterans, Near Castlemaine, Victoria c.1930s
nla.cat-vn1987582

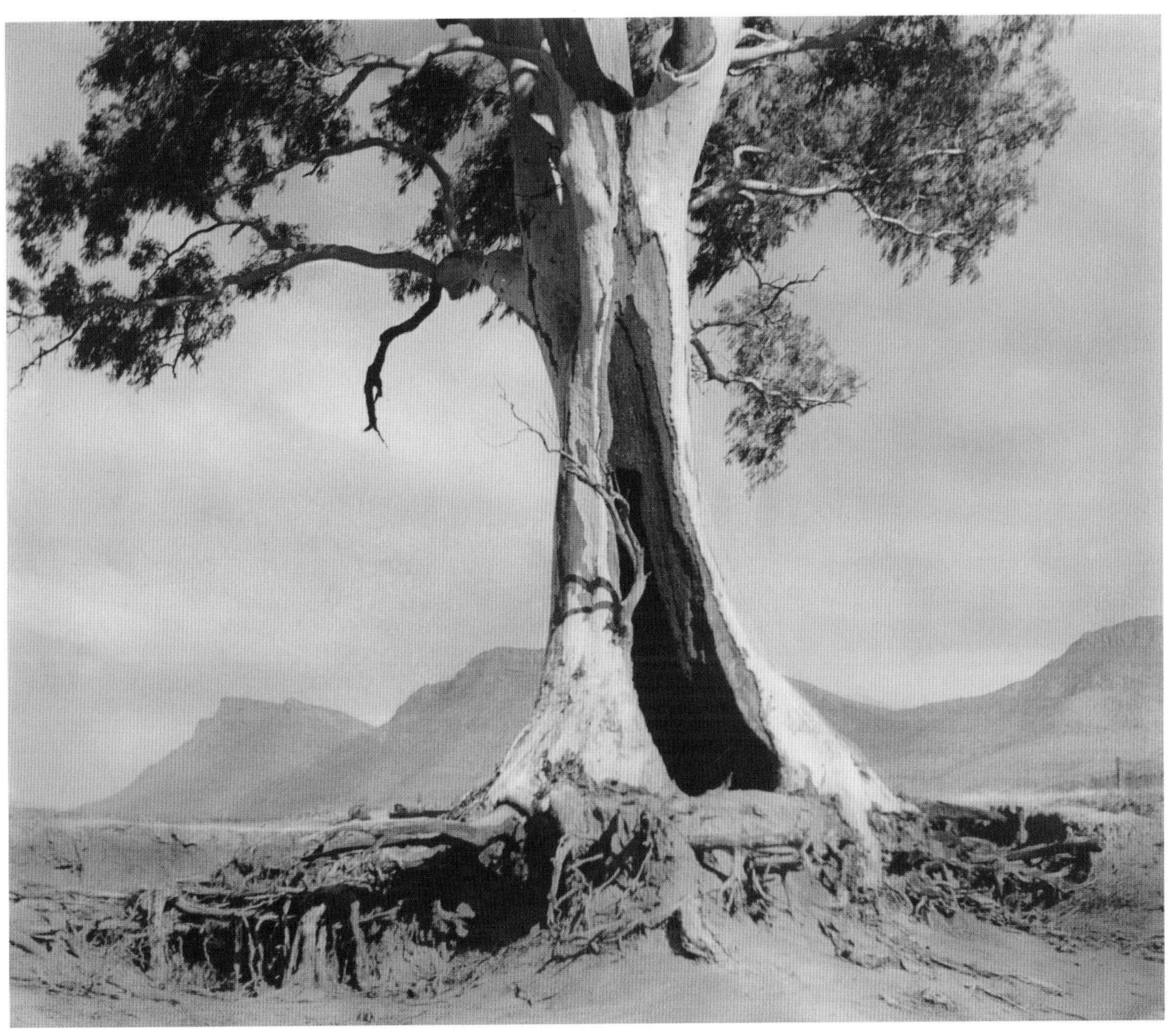

Spirit of Endurance 1937
nla.cat-vn1987383

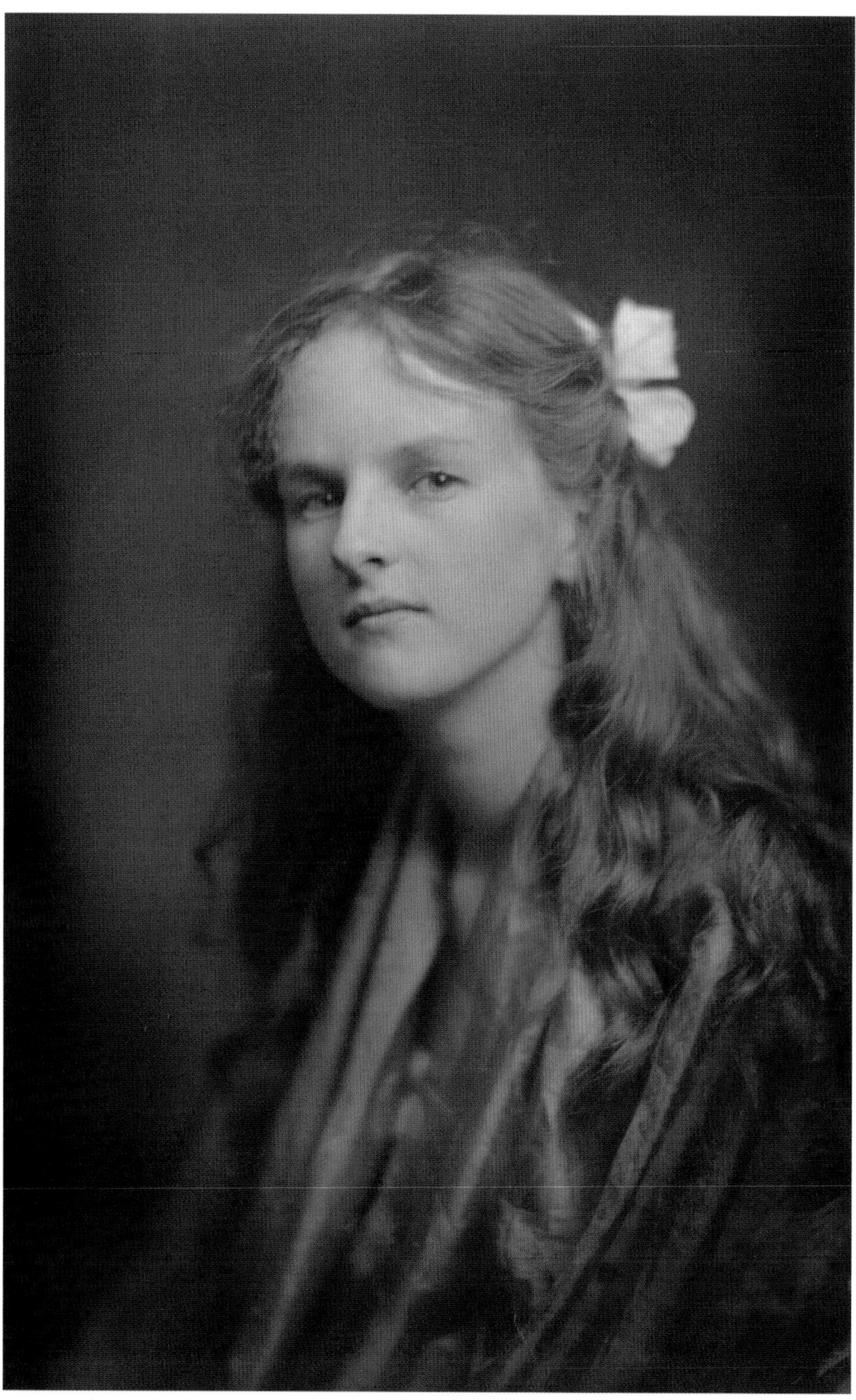

Portrait of My Cousin 1906
nla.cat-vn3044977

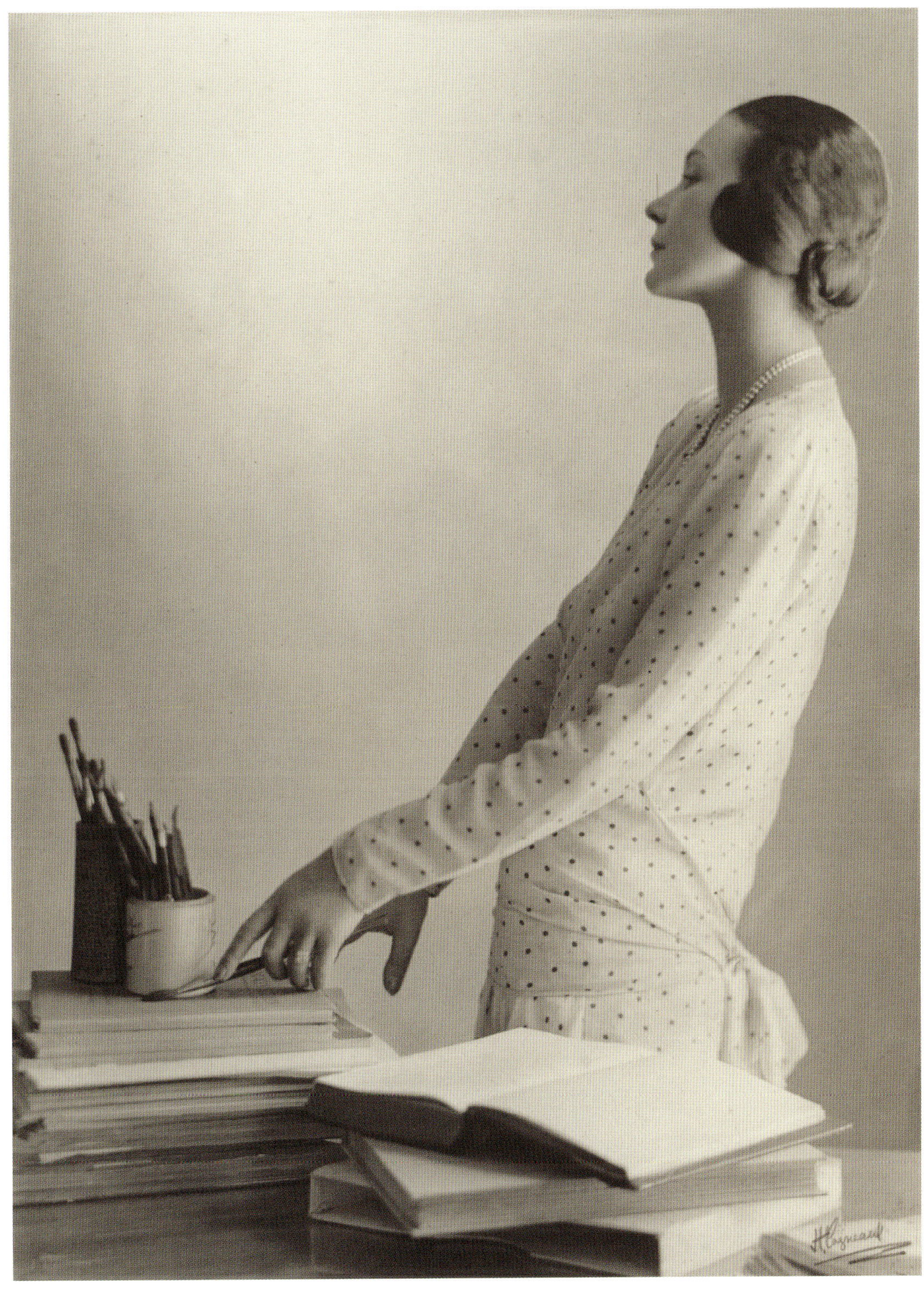

Doris Zinkeison [ie. Zinkeisen] 1930
nla.cat-vn1986848

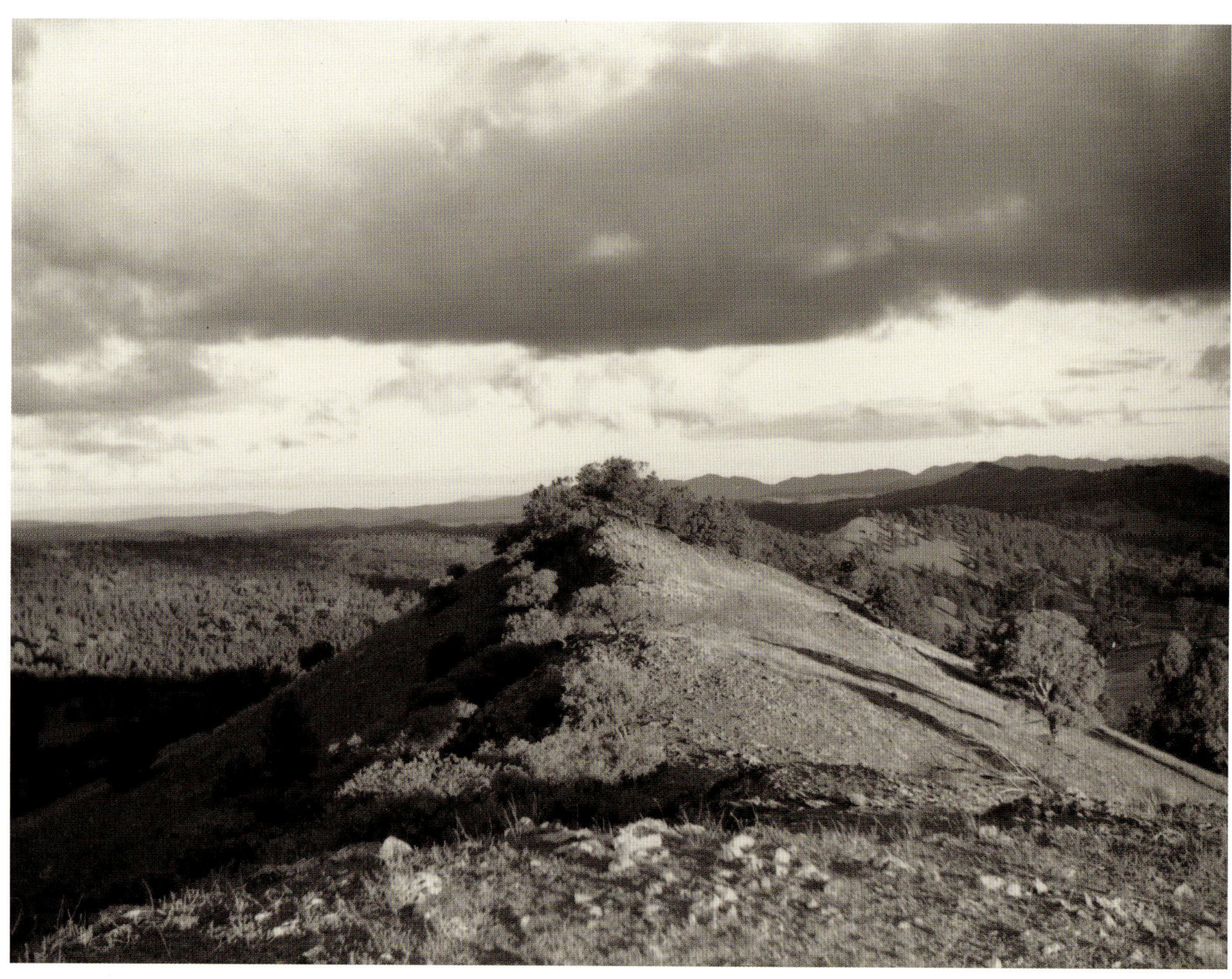

Far flung Ranges of the Flinders 1937
nla.cat-vn3044977

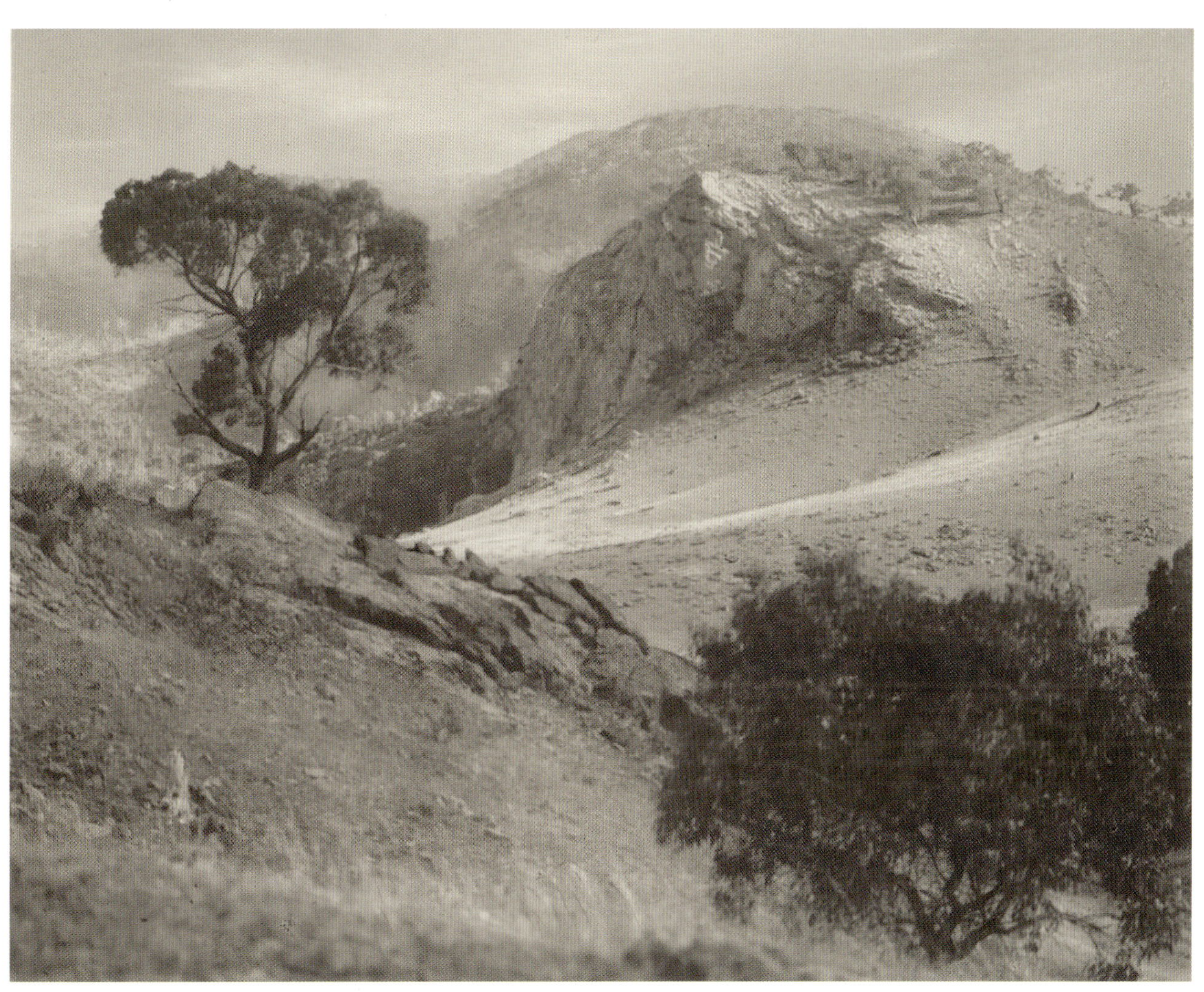

The Valley, Sofala, New South Wales 1925
nla.cat-vn1987560

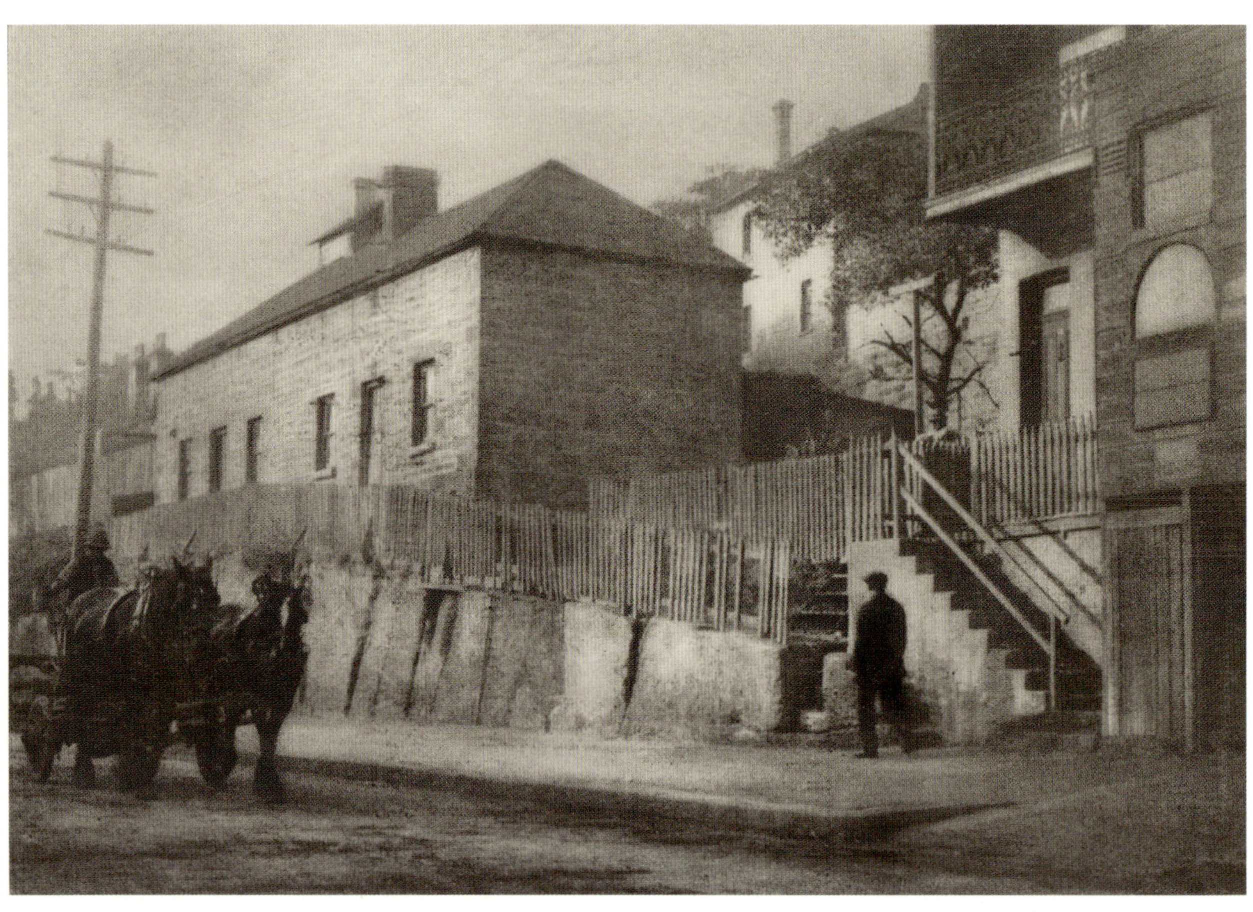

Kent Street, Old Sydney 1911
nla.cat-vn464610

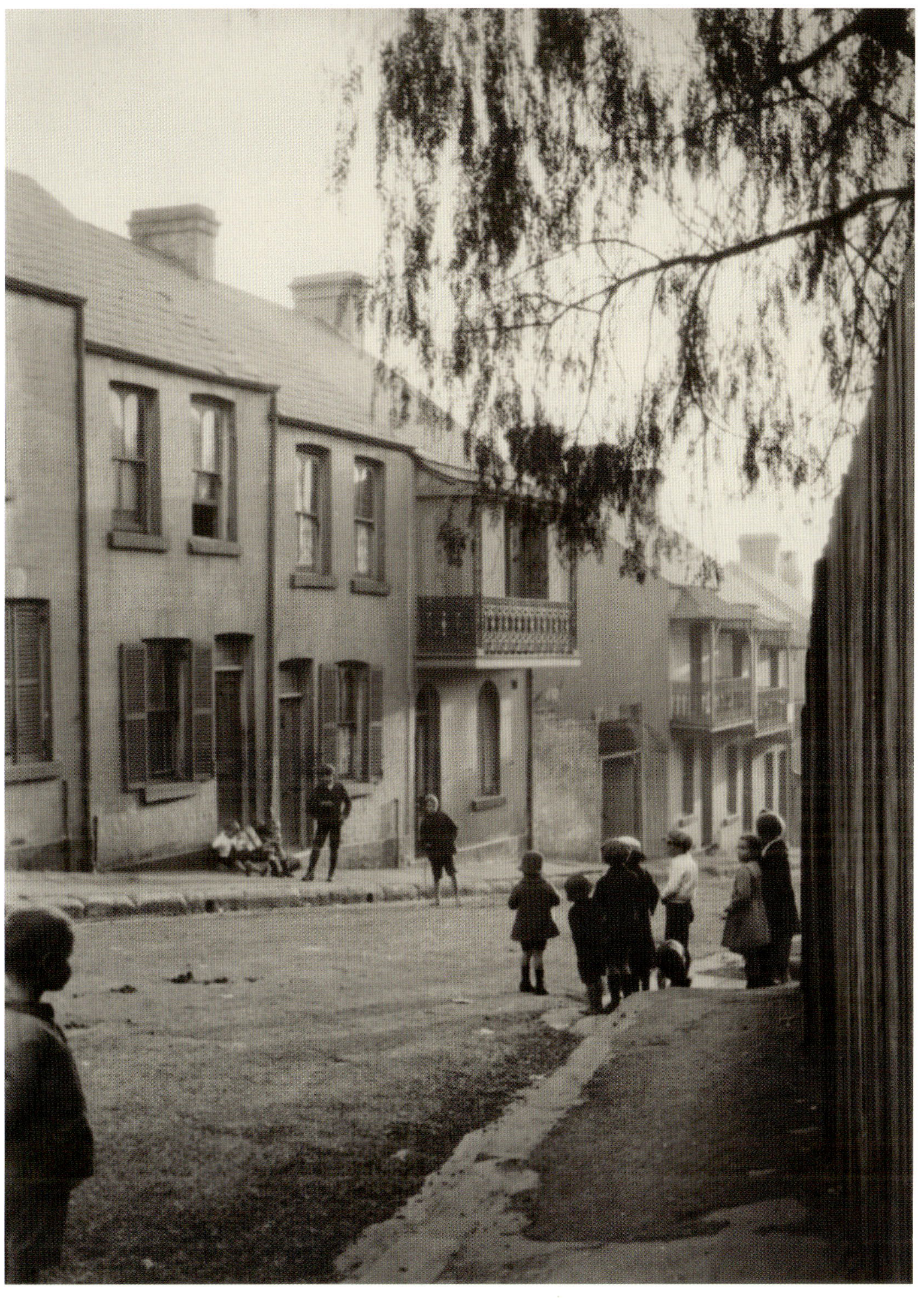

Old Streets, East Sydney 1911
nla.cat-vn443064

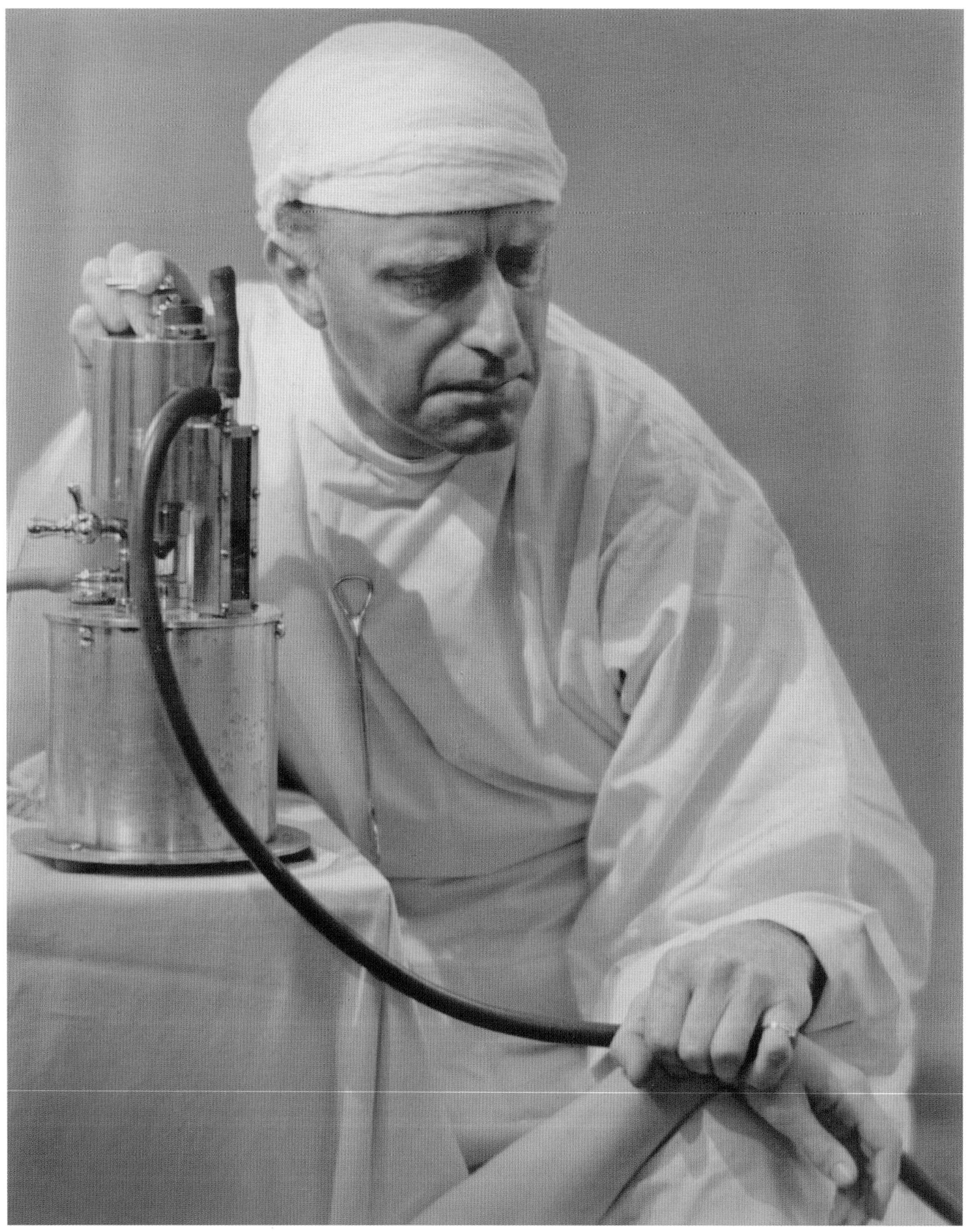

The Anaesthetist 1933
nla.cat-vn464091

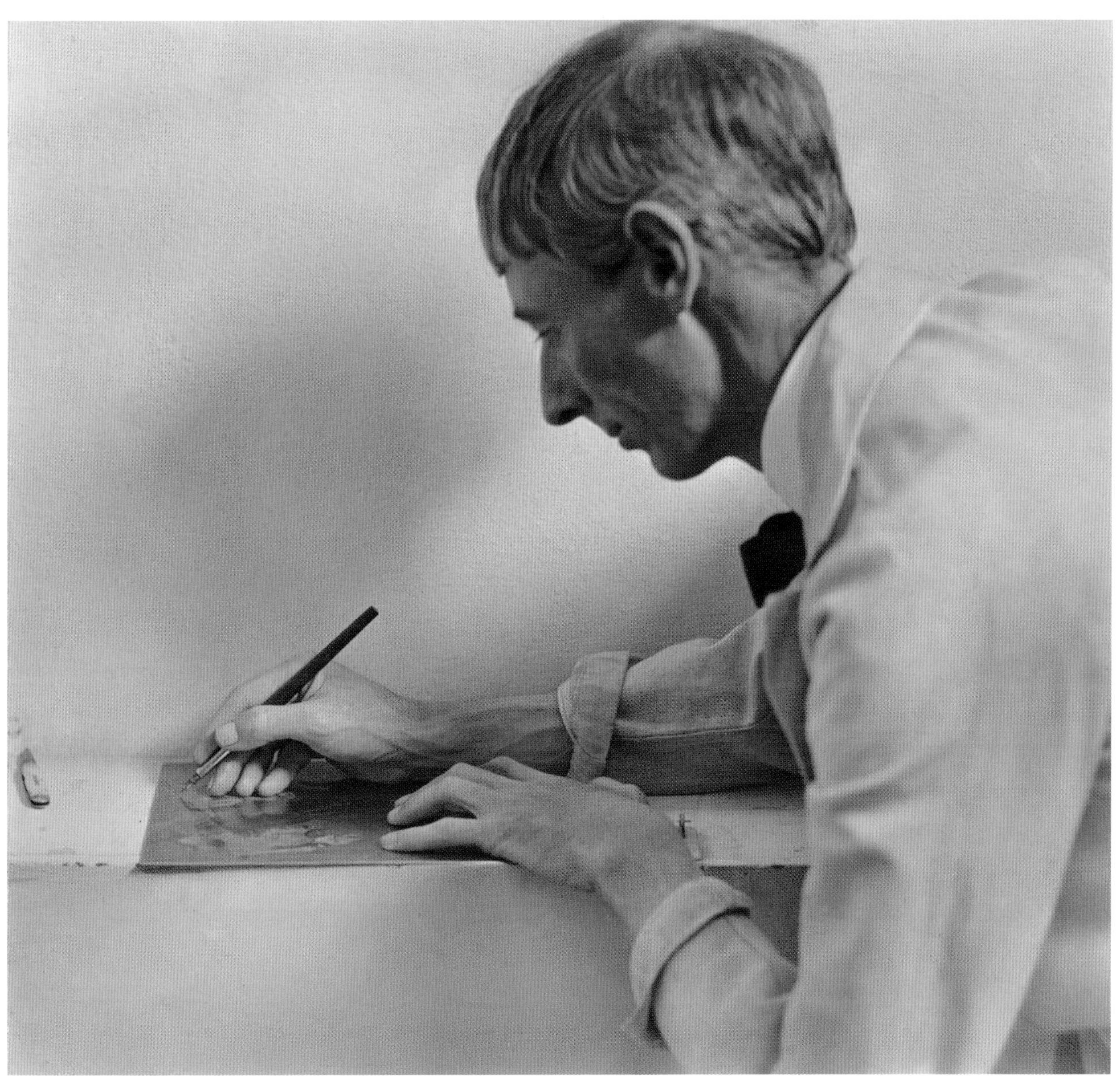

The Etcher, Norman Lindsay c.1930
nla.cat-vn464319

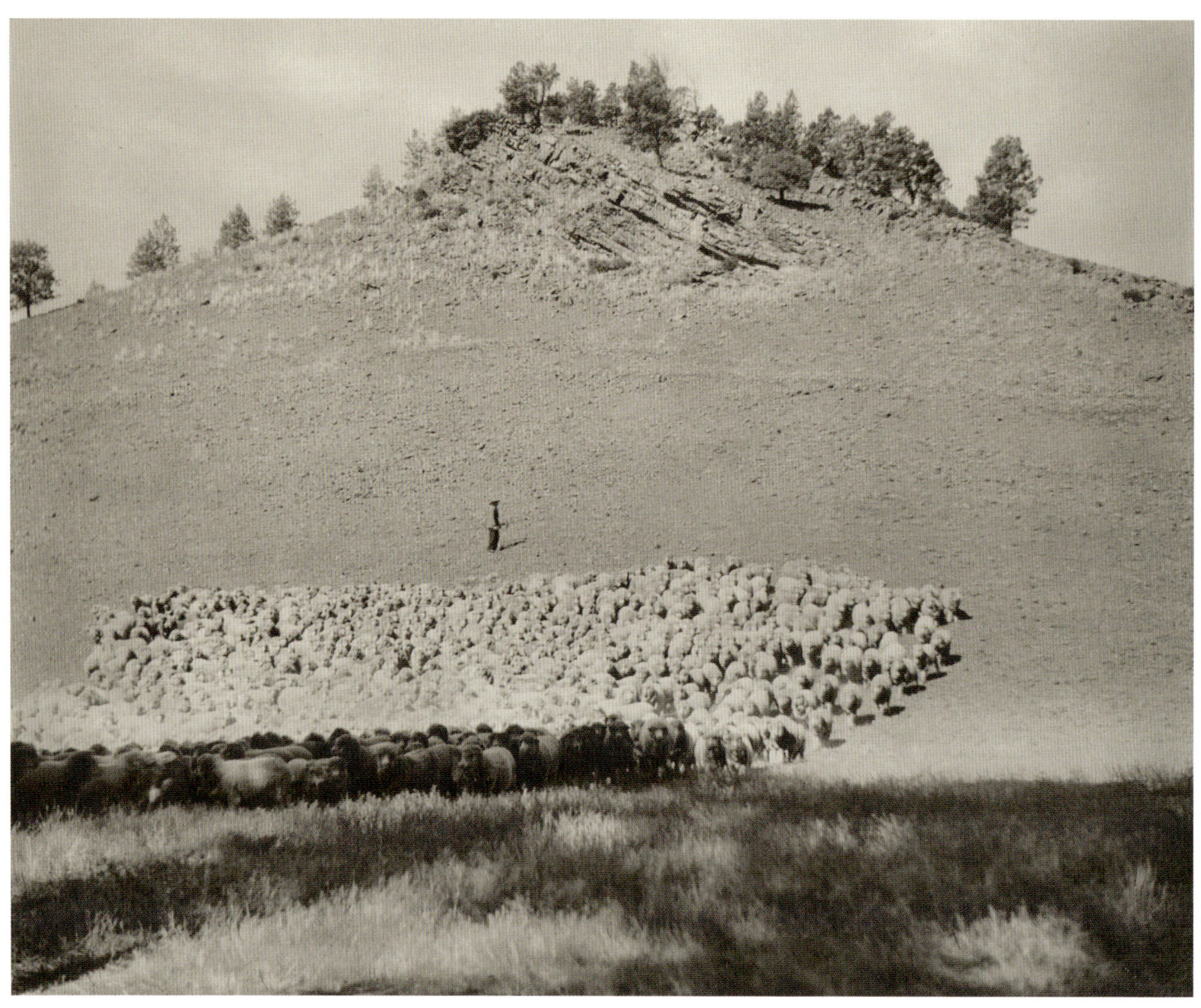

Mustering Sheep, Flinders Ranges, South Australia c.1937
nla.cat-vn464915

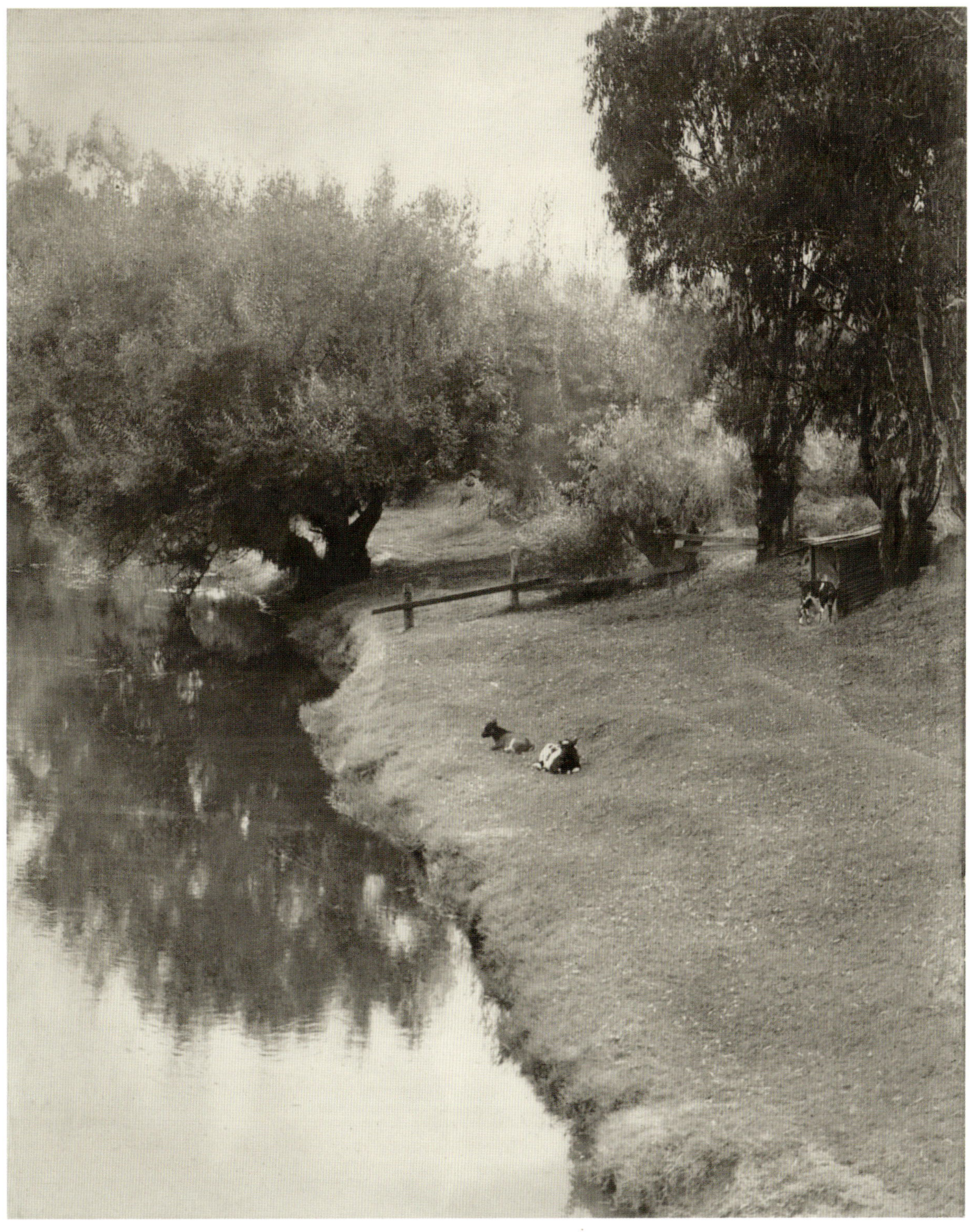

River Pastoral c.1935
nla.cat-vn1987375

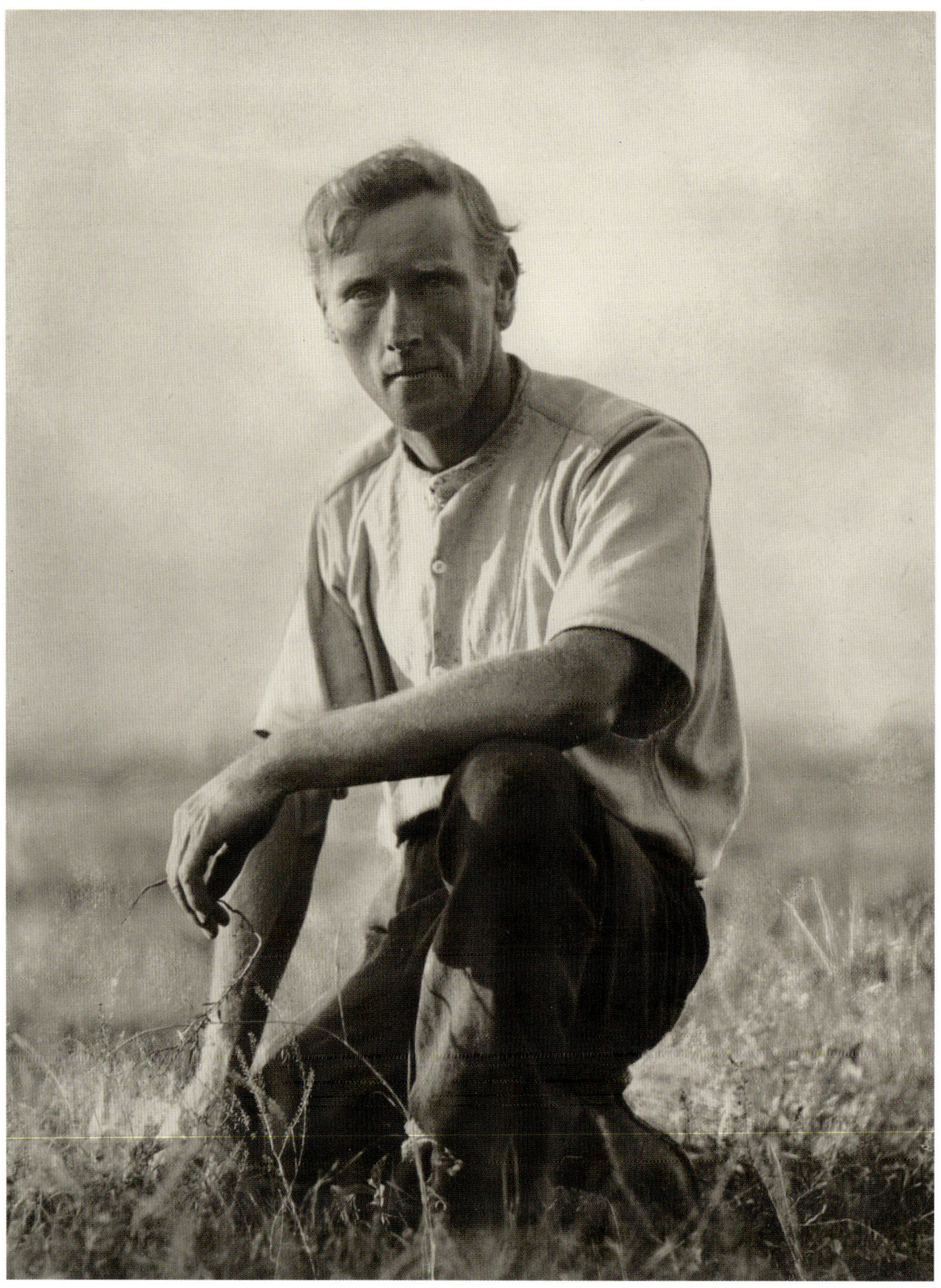

Son of the Soil between 1920 and 1929
nla.cat-vn464037